THE WOMAN NEXT DOOR

*One woman's story of capture
& eventual escape from the clutches
of domestic violence & madness.*

EVE STRONGHEART

The Woman Next Door
Copyright © 2017 by Eve Strongheart

No part of this publication may be reproduced, distributed, or transmitted in any form or by any means, including photocopying, recording, or other electronic or mechanical methods, without the prior written permission of the author, except in the case of brief quotations embodied in critical reviews and certain other non-commercial uses permitted by copyright law.

Tellwell Talent
www.tellwell.ca
ISBN
978-1-77370-250-6 (Hardcover)
978-1-77370-249-0 (Paperback)

To Sherry,
Thank you.

Table of Contents

Introduction

I tried to write this story once before, without delving into the more intimate and personal aspects of my tale. I had planned to publish this narrative anonymously, but still I found myself avoiding a complete and full disclosure regarding some of its aspects. They were so personal, so private, and they were, in so many ways, so humiliating. Yet I discovered that, without those parts of my story, the rest of it doesn't really add up. I have found that it is impossible to share my tale accurately without sharing all of it.

For this reason, I am writing this story again, unedited, with all the details I find embarrassing included. I have a dual purpose in trying to share this tale. My main purpose is an attempt to help someone else avoid the prolonged pain and near self-destruction which I experienced. My second purpose is a personal search for closure, for understanding, and, ultimately, for peace.

I have considered many titles for this book. One title could be: "How did a nice woman like me wind up in a mess like that?" Another title could be, perhaps: "Don't fall into the same trap I did." The most succinct title would probably be: "I thought I was smarter."

What I know today is that an intelligent, educated, independent, and resourceful woman can wind up hopelessly entangled in a relationship so confusing that she falls into despair. I know that it is possible to become so lost that one cannot see the way out, or even imagine that there is one. I know it is possible for an unhealthy relationship to drive a woman to the edge of self-destruction, to a place where she can lose all sense of self, and allow all of her boundaries to collapse, one by one. I know that, step by step, a woman can get to a place where she hardly recognizes herself. I know all this because it happened to me. Finding my way back took patience, courage, determination, self-forgiveness, and the support of another woman who understood.

If you think you may be heading down a similar road, please stop for a moment and read my tale. Perhaps I can be that person for you; the one who understands. Because it doesn't get any easier to leave the longer you stay.

Chapter One

What set me up

Once, when I was a teenager, I got lost in a forest. I had gone backpacking with a friend, and, being young and of an adventurous spirit, we left the established trail to strike off on our own, trying to make it to a beautiful mountain lake which glimmered in the distance. Hiking through the brush became harder and harder the further we went, and, by the time we realized we could not reach our destination, we were hopelessly lost. Hours of trudging through the woods got us no closer, until finally I looked down and saw my own boot print in the mud, headed in the opposite direction from which I was traveling. I had hiked in a large circle and then doubled back on myself without even knowing it.

This misguided backpacking trip turned out to be a perfect metaphor for my emotionally abusive marriage. By the time I realized I was in trouble, I had lost all sense of direction, all sense of which was the right path to take, and all confidence in my own judgement. Attempts to solve my problem with counseling and other means just made the situation worse and only left me more confused and exhausted. I have learned that once you realize you are lost, it is important to slow down and conserve your energy. Getting out is more likely to require a prolonged and carefully planned marathon rather than a quick sprint. This is the story of how I got lost in the wilderness of an abusive marriage and how I slowly found my way back out again.

I could be the woman who lives next door. My situation does not look that dramatic from the outside. You will not see me covered in bruises, or wearing casts to help heal broken bones. My husband hits me with words. He hits me secretly, in the most private places. It is important to him that other people think he is a "nice guy." Only I know the truth. For those who have survived physical assault it may not look that bad, and I can understand that for women who have lived through those horrors, anything less seems insignificant. But there are many of us out there who are secretly broken. I can guarantee you that it does not take physical assault to leave a woman lost in the depths of despair. I know that sometimes I thought it would have been easier if he hit me with his fists instead of his words; at least then I would have understood why I was in so much pain. I believe my body is tougher than my heart and spirit turned out to be. I believe that every woman's hurts are personal to her, and I know that often an abuser knows just where the soft spot is on his victim. We all have our weaknesses, our vulnerabilities. With our loved ones, these tender spots are supposed to be safe, protected, understood. An abuser sees these areas as an easy target, a place to inflict pain in order to gain control. One woman may be sensitive about her body, so he says: "You are a fat, ugly cow." These are the words he knows will hurt her the most. Another woman may be sensitive about her sexuality, so he will call her frigid or a whore. The names grow viler the longer she stays.

People sometimes do not understand why a woman might stay with a man who is abusive. They say: "If it is so bad, why doesn't she just leave?" But it is hard to walk away when one's emotional legs have been broken. The first blows in domestic violence are directed at a woman's confidence, sense of self, and independence. By their very nature, emotional and verbal abuse are designed to disable and disarm the victim on the first strike, so that she cannot fight back.

I believe bullies and abusers are essentially cowards. It is never a fair fight. By the time the real abuse starts, women have often been separated from their support systems; they have been isolated. Abusers will do this early on in the relationship, when things are still good. It is done in the name of love. A man might say: "Why don't you quit your job? They don't appreciate you like I do. Move in with me so that we can have more time together, I love you so much." These words, which sound so loving, can be the first bars of a carefully constructed cage designed to keep a woman hostage.

As for me, my story begins after years of experience as a counselor, first working in the field of alcohol and drug counseling, and then, in later years, working in the field of mental health. I am well qualified for these jobs, having a Bachelor of Science degree in Psychology and a Master of Science degree in Counseling. You would think I would know better. You would think I would have the wisdom and the self-respect to not fall into the trap which later ensnared me. Looking back on the whole story now, I realize that several factors contributed to what happened to me.

I believe many women fall into the hands of an abuser through a variety of circumstances which make them vulnerable. These could include a very sheltered upbringing or an abusive one. A woman might have a sick child or health problems of her own. Economic factors such as poverty or the stress of the working poor are other reasons women get trapped. There are also cultural and religious philosophies which can teach a woman to be subservient to men. The sad truth is that abusive men seek out women who are vulnerable; it is their very nature to do so. This is the tale of how it happened to me.

At the age of forty-three, I decided to make a big change in my life. Actually, the decision had been slowly building for years, and as these things often happen, I finally came to a fork in the road. I lived in the far north, in Alaska, and it was time to move south to a warmer climate. I had been having trouble with the darkness, the cold, and the ice for many years. But the only family I had lived in Alaska, and moving south where I did not know anyone was a daunting prospect. To further complicate things, I wanted to move back to my native Canada, where I had not lived since I was a young child. I had dual citizenship, and felt a call to return to the land of my birth. This meant moving to a different country where I had no ties, had never worked, had no credit history, and knew no one.

Eventually, my discomfort with the long winters outweighed the fear of striking off on my own. I packed up my things, put my house on the market, moved into a thirty-one-foot motorhome with a dog and two cats for company, and began the drive south. I had never before driven anything that big, and was also towing my car. In addition, I had a two-person, ocean-going kayak strapped to the top of my car. Needless to say, I was extremely intimidated by what I was trying to do, but I told myself that not being able to do it was not an option. Gradually I made my way south, at first going much slower than the speed limit, with angry cars backing up behind me. Eventually I gained confidence and speed, and the miles began to slip by. I discovered that driving something that long required a special technique. At first I was weaving back and forth across the road, moving more like a fish than a car. Somehow the idea came to me that it was like cutting out fabric when sewing one's own clothes. If a person looks just ahead of the scissors, the cut will not be straight; however, if the seamstress looks ahead along the line of the cut, a straight line can be achieved. I found that if I looked farther down the road ahead of me, I was able to avoid over-correcting and thus drove in a straight line. It took me hundreds of miles to figure this out.

I came to the border and completed the paperwork to immigrate back to Canada. I told the customs agent that I had a job waiting for me in southern British Columbia, which I did. While attending a conference in Alaska at which I had been a speaker, I had met some people who were there promoting a private drug and alcohol treatment program in B.C. We had many discussions over the course of a few days and they had eventually offered me a job. Everything seemed to be lining up quite nicely to make my dream of returning home a reality.

After a little more than a week, I wound up at my destination, a place I like to think of as my First Landing. My new job was at a residential treatment facility which promoted itself as the client's Last Chance, and they had promised me a position as one of their counselors. They had also helped me locate a campground near the treatment centre where I could live year-round in my motorhome. The situation suited me and my animals perfectly. We had power and showers in the campground, and I was only five minutes away from my new place of employment. I would be able to come home at lunch time to check on my dog and cats. I was content.

This new job turned out to be stressful and demanding. The program was privately owned and had about one hundred clients living there at a time. The owner was a woman who treated staff more like her personal playthings than employees. I soon realized that there was a significant amount of dysfunction going on at Last Chance. I made friends at work quickly with another counselor; however, my clinical supervisor warned me off from this relationship, telling me that this woman was "not my peer." Shortly afterward, my new friend was fired, and I suddenly realized I would have to watch my back at work. It was a very toxic environment. The owner actually told us in one of our daily staff meetings that she could get trained monkeys to do our jobs. I had a Master's degree and over twenty years of experience, so I knew this was not true. Still, I needed the job; so I kept my mouth shut. I realized I had moved over three thousand miles to land in a snake pit.

I was now living in a town where I knew no one and I could not make friends at work. It was too difficult to know whom to trust among the staff. Many of them were completely under the sway of our megalomaniac boss. I realized some were not really qualified for their jobs; perhaps being over their heads made them doubt themselves. Outside loyalties were frowned upon. One staff member was actually forced to come back from his honeymoon to attend one of these unpaid staff meetings. He had made the mistake of answering the phone.

I felt trapped for my own reasons. I had moved a long way to take this job, and it was my first and only one in Canada. In addition, when I first arrived I had been forced to sign a non-competition agreement. This stated that I would not work at any similar facility within a hundred mile radius of Last Chance for at least two years after ending my employment there. In other words, if I quit my job, I either had to give up my profession and find another field of work, or I had to move again. I did not know how things were normally done in Canada. I found out later that this requirement was completely outside the norm and illegal. I have since worked for many fine companies in this country, however at the time, I was a recent immigrant and very vulnerable.

The level of emotional abuse directed at staff was unbelievable. Driving back up north, however, did not feel like an option, and so I had nowhere else to go. Needless to say, I tried to find a way to make it work, keeping my head down and trying to avoid the attention of our boss. I was good at what I did and the clients liked me, so I found a way to stay out of the line of fire by keeping my opinions to myself. Still, it was lonely having no friends or even acquaintances with whom I could spend my free time. I did not dare socialize with my co-workers, for fear that, in an unguarded moment, I might say or do something which would cause me problems at work. Through observation, I had learned that the only safe place to be was off to the sidelines, out of sight. People who became the focus of her attention wound up being pinned like a bug and examined under the microscope of her bright but disturbed mind.

I began to look for other ways to meet people. Since I had brought a kayak with me, kayaking was a logical place to start. Unfortunately, it was a two-person craft, so I could not go out by myself; it was too heavy to lift and too big for me to maneuver. I began to look around for ways to meet someone with whom I could go kayaking. One day, after living in First Landing for about two months, I saw an ad in the local newspaper's personal column placed by a man my age who was looking for companionship, and he specifically made a reference to kayaking as something he liked to do. I decided to respond. It wasn't long before we began communicating. I found out that he lived in another town about seventy-five miles away from me. This sounded absolutely perfect. I was nervous about becoming too involved with someone, and was just looking for a friend with whom I could occasionally get together for outdoor adventures. Seventy-five miles away sounded just about right.

Frank and I spoke on the phone many times, and we seemed to get along well. We had many areas of common interest, mostly a love of the outdoors, camping, and animals. He had been divorced for five years and had two young children, an eight year-old son named Tommy and a fifteen year-old one named Mark. He told me that his wife of fourteen years divorced him when he was injured in a car accident. He said he had acquired a mild brain injury and he had been off work for a while after the accident. He said he was now back at work and doing fine. He described himself as a good man who was abandoned by his wife when he was injured and temporarily unable to work. I believed him and felt sorry for him.

I spoke with Frank for several weeks on the phone. He seemed polite, well mannered, intelligent, charming, and we found plenty to talk about. Eventually, we decided to meet for dinner, and I drove the seventy-five miles to his town to meet at a restaurant. I brought along my large, male German shepherd as a sort of bodyguard. We had not exchanged photos, so it was a real blind date, but when I met him he seemed to be everything he had presented himself to be. He was tall, good looking, well groomed, and well dressed. After a pleasant dinner, we took my dog for a long walk. When we finally got back to my car, we found out that I had received a parking ticket. I was used to living in rural Alaska, and when I had parked in the large empty lot it did not occur to me that I would have to pay for parking. He quickly scooped up the ticket, and insisted on taking care of it for me. What a gentleman! I began to feel like I was a little out of my element in this big city.

We met again for dinner the following weekend, after talking nightly on the phone all week. This time we met at a town halfway between us, which seemed fair. After another lovely meal and another walk, we were saying our goodbyes in the parking lot. What happened next was my first clue of what was to come, but I missed the warning; I didn't pay attention to the signs, and I kept walking right into a trap.

He asked me what I would like to do next. By now we had met for dinner twice, gone for two long walks, and had spoken nightly on the phone for several weeks. During this time, a focus of our discussions had been on our mutual love of camping and the outdoors. He had lived his whole life in the area, and he had told me about many wonderful spots nearby. So I suggested that we go camping. This turned out to be the wrong thing to say. After I said this, he stiffened, and in a very disapproving tone said that that was rather presumptuous of me. I quickly and vehemently began to protest that there was nothing presumptuous about it. I stated that I had gone camping with many people on a strictly platonic basis. I was quite insulted by his insinuation and I told him so. His response was to kiss me.

This first kiss established a pattern which was to last throughout our relationship. I would innocently say or do something of which he did not approve, and he would unexpectedly give me a strong reprimand. He would then follow it by a gesture of affection. It made my head spin. It kept me perpetually off balance. Throughout our relationship, he seemed to have an uncanny sense of how far he could push me. Just when I had reached my breaking point, he would reel me back in like a fish on a line, with expressions of love and devotion. What is particularly troubling to me in retrospect is that as a result of this, my boundaries seemed to move. It was like huge waves constantly crashing on a shoreline, gradually wearing it down. After each incident, I would regroup and get my feet back under me emotionally. What I didn't realize until much later was that my boundaries moved slightly each time. The type of behaviour which I would tolerate had shifted. After years of this onslaught, I hardly recognized myself. The abuse in my marriage was like death by a thousand cuts. Each cut was minor in itself; I only lost a teaspoon of blood each time. Over time, however, and by the sheer volume of incidents, I became worn down, weak, confused. I went from being a strong woman with reasonable self-confidence to an emotionally battered wreck. To this day, I don't know if this tactic was premeditated or just an ingrained pattern of behaviour, the only way he knew how to relate to a romantic partner. What I do know is that the constant change in direction confused me, kept me off balance, and made me doubt myself and my reactions. This doubt and confusion lasted for over nine years.

Chapter Two

Doubting myself

They don't teach you anything about domestic violence when you are getting a degree in counseling. You would think they would, but the program I completed in 1991 didn't include it. Despite my education and my experience, I was completely unprepared for what I was about to encounter.

Once Frank and I started officially dating, the process of slowly undermining my confidence began. At first it was subtle, done under the guise of being "helpful." Frank began giving me gifts of shampoo, conditioner, and face cream. He never gave me the products I used, but instead substituted products he said were better. At first, this seemed nice, an attempt to be thoughtful; but after a while, the message I received was that my choices were wrong, and that he knew better than I. This became apparent when I tried to protest his changes by telling him that I preferred the products I had chosen. Being prone to allergies and skin rashes, I had to find products to which I did not react and stick with them. I tried to explain this to him, but he insisted he was just trying to pamper me and he continued buying products I didn't want to use, filling up my small trailer with them. Face cream, moisturizer, mascara, razors, shaving cream, shampoo, soap, all of my most personal toiletries were reviewed and changed. He even disagreed with the type of feminine hygiene product I used, wanting me to use a different brand. I was finally able to assert that he could know nothing about this and I continued to use the brand I preferred, but despite (or perhaps because of) this small victory, I was assailed on every other front.

The campaign to get me to change was subtle but endless. At first, I tried to accept his gifts in good grace, but when it became too much and I tried to push back, he quietly informed me that I had been living in the back woods for too long, that I was uninformed, unsophisticated, and backward. He told me it was OK because he would help me know how to do things properly. He knew I was very sensitive about being an immigrant. I wanted so much to fit in to my homeland. I had been living in a rural area of Alaska for thirty-three years. Now I was home and that meant a lot to me. I wanted to put down roots and truly belong somewhere at last. When he would tell me repeatedly that wasn't the way things were done in Canada, he had my full attention. Gifts can be a lovely gesture of affection, but if a man gives a woman toiletries to which she might be allergic and then criticizes her for not using them, it becomes something else. When he does it with a smile and a teasing energy, it is hard to know what to think. Looking back now I realize I should have run when he first began to undermine my confidence this way. Unfortunately, I didn't run. Where was I going to go? To whom was I going to talk? I was isolated, and that made me vulnerable. Besides, if I had complained about this man giving me unwelcome gifts, I might not have found much sympathy. It is only when the pervasive pattern emerges that the impact can be seen.

Just like waves crashing on a shore line, wearing it down, he challenged my boundaries on every side. I wondered: "Why am I so annoyed when he is just trying to be nice? What is wrong with me? Am I really that backward? Have I really lost all sense of how things are done in polite society?" Whenever he saw my confidence shift a little, he moved right in and focused on changing that one part of me. It was insidious.

After a while, his intrusions continued onto the next layer of my person. He gave me different underwear which he said was healthier for me. He bought me expensive lingerie, but it was always a couple of sizes too small. He loved to shop at a boutique lingerie store which catered to young women. I am sure the sales clerks there thought that the woman for whom he was buying these gifts was a lucky lady indeed. But I could never wear what he purchased. It never fit. One can imagine the message I received here. I was supposed to be sexier, smaller, and younger. These gifts were given with a smile, so what did it mean? What was wrong with me that I didn't like it? I was constantly trying to fend off an encroaching invasion of my person and my boundaries. He told me that I had just never had anyone love me before. I wondered, however, if this was love. Was there really something wrong with me because I didn't like it?

I also noticed right away that there was something about our sex life which made me uncomfortable. It was hard to identify, but it seemed like some kind of ongoing power struggle. He would insist on touching me in ways which I did not enjoy, and then expect me to somehow change what I liked in order to accommodate him. For example, he wanted to pay far too much attention to my nipples, which are sensitive. When I told him that after a while it would start to hurt instead of feeling good, he would just recommend a certain cream he thought I should use, which he said would solve the problem. He believed he knew my body better than I did, and I was expected to adjust. When I tried to explain that a cream would not change my basic wiring, he just continued to push me to use it. This particular issue was a point of contention throughout the nine years of our relationship. There was an ongoing power struggle in our sex life which I found very confusing.

We started spending every weekend together, alternating one at my place and the other at his. I gave him a key to my trailer and if I came home late on Friday night I would find him cleaning. It was nice having someone help at first, but many times, he went too far. My motorhome was thirty-one feet long. Since I was sharing it with a large dog and two cats, there wasn't a lot of room. And yet, he began leaving things at my place. When I asked him to take them home with him because I really didn't have room to store them, he argued, relentlessly. I felt that he was marking his territory, but he denied any such motivation.

I felt guilty for asking him to take his pajamas home after every visit; he wanted to leave them hanging on a hook in my motorhome. But there just wasn't enough space, and I really didn't think it was that big of a deal.

Another conflict over territory came up over Christmas. He knew that I had not planned on decorating for the holidays, which were fast approaching. Living in a trailer with space at a premium, it was hard to find room for everything, and I am a tidy person by nature who prefers uncluttered surroundings. I also was not really in the mood at that point in my life. I was going to have to work over the holidays, including on Christmas Day, which, combined with the toxic atmosphere at my job, killed any sense of festivity. Nevertheless, I came home from work one day to find that he had decorated the inside of my crowded trailer by hanging baubles and lights everywhere. I hit my head on them when I walked down the corridor. To me, it just added clutter and chaos to an already small and crowded space, but he defended the decorations by saying he was just trying to bring a little Christmas into my life. What kind of a person was I if I complained about that?

One thing that had rather surprised me was how quickly Frank had chosen to introduce me to his children. I thought most single parents would shield their children from their dating life, but he introduced me to his kids on our third date. I realize now it was part of a rush to attain intimacy and further our involvement. He realized I was isolated, alone, and lonely. Meeting his children quickly increased our connection, as it gave me the sense of family I was missing. To further intensify this effect, I wound up really bonding with his youngest son, Tommy. His elder son, Mark, was fifteen and not interested in forming a connection with another adult. For him, life was all about his friends, which of course was completely normal. Tommy, however, was cute, and the lowest on the pecking order in his family. My nurturing side was triggered by someone who seemed to need a champion. Frank was caught up in trying to appease his eldest son's moods, which often left Tommy and I to our own devices during my visits.

Frank required that his children do chores, and this area gave me another clue, which I missed, of what was to come. I noticed a pattern after a while regarding the children's chores. Doing dishes was their responsibility, since their father cooked, and I noticed that his eldest son Mark would "put off" doing the dishes when it was his turn. In his efforts to appease him, Frank would allow this, but I noticed that often Mark would put them off until another mealtime had passed, and then it would be Tommy's turn again, who would wind up having to do both sets of dishes. Tommy was on the small side for eight years old. When it was his turn to do the dishes, he required a stool to comfortably reach the sink. Seeing this small boy standing on a stool starting on the big pile of dishes touched my heart, and of course I would help him.

His father did not seem to notice the inequity. After watching this pattern unfold repeatedly over many visits, I eventually said something to Frank. He went to have a talk with Mark. I do not know what he said to him, but it led to a big fight between them that caused Mark to end his visits with his father. This did not help my relationship with Mark at all. Looking back, I realize that Mark stood up to his father in a way that Tommy and I did not. I now admire him for that, but at the time, I did not know what to think of their conflict. Not having children of my own, I deferred too much to Frank's judgement. I often doubted evidence that was right before my eyes.

Mark was at an age when he was no longer required to visit his father as part of his parents' divorce agreement, and he began exercising this right. Soon it was just Tommy, Frank, and I on my visits. Tommy seemed to like his rise in the social hierarchy, and our bond deepened. My love for this young boy contributed to my entrapment. He was a very effective lure for a childless woman, and a big part of the reason I stayed in the relationship as long as I did. I think Frank was well aware of the effectiveness of this incentive, and he encouraged this bond between us. It played to his advantage.

My job continued to be very stressful, and the situation there deteriorated. The owner of the company would periodically keep us after work for marathon staff meeting during which we would be criticized for the lack of progress of our clients, or for any client who had walked out of treatment—both of which were, most of the time, out of our control. On one occasion, we were required to go around the room and rate each other's performance. We were required to literally give a "thumbs up," or a "thumbs down" judging our fellow staff members on their commitment to the job. In this way, each person was scored by the group. I quickly observed that if any staff member gave a "thumbs up" to everyone, he or she would become the focus of the next attack, being criticized for not taking the exercise seriously, etc. We were thus required to throw some of our co-workers under the bus, so to speak, or else we would become the focus of a brutal inquest. It was quite a shocking experience for me to watch these staff meeting tactics. I knew the whole situation was completely dysfunctional, but what could I do about it? I didn't want to move back up north, and, with the non-competition agreement I was forced to sign, quitting this job would mean moving again.

Looking back, I now realize how much this employment situation contributed to my developing a relationship with Frank. I had moved three thousand miles away from everything familiar. I was in a country which was new to me as an adult. I had little time or opportunity to meet people outside of work, and forming friendships with clients was off limits. The politics at my place of employment kept me from forming real relationships with my co-workers, especially after the one woman I had trusted was fired. I had carefully watched the dynamics among my co-workers. I saw a couple of the other counselors try to talk to the owner about the dysfunctional aspects of our staff meetings and general staff morale. These turned out to be suicide missions. Since she was the one running our "staff meetings," she thought everything she did was perfect; their suggestions instantly branded them as traitors.

To further complicate things, since we were a drug and alcohol addiction treatment centre, several of our staff, including myself, were people in recovery, meaning we used to have an alcohol or a drug problem, but we were now sober. People who have beaten their own addiction oftentimes want to help someone else, and so they go back to school to become counselors. This was my story as well. As the owner of our treatment centre could not listen to criticism of any kind, people who told her she was less than perfect became immediately suspect, and another tactic she would use was to decide that they were obviously in relapse, meaning they had started to drink or use drugs again. It was clear to me that this was not the case, but still she effectively ruined their reputations, telling everyone that they had relapsed. For a drug and alcohol counselor in recovery, this is the kiss of death to that person's career. Any staff member who tried to speak up would very soon after either quit or be fired, and their reputation was thoroughly destroyed after they had left.

It was at this point that I decided I was in serious trouble. My new job at this fancy treatment center could lead to the end of my career if I wasn't careful. I realized that speaking honestly and openly about my opinions was a path I dared not take. I started to be even more careful about what I said to my co-workers, and of course I would never voice my personal problems to clients. Frank became my only confidant. The town I was living in was small, only 50,000 people, and the treatment center was big news in town. Many former clients who completed the program successfully relocated there to stay close to the treatment center, which encouraged continued contact after graduation for clients who stayed sober. As soon as it was heard that a client had relapsed, he or she was banned from the treatment center and any of their support meetings. In this way, our program became like an exclusive club with strict admission criteria. No one wanted to be kicked out. Being a recovering person myself, I should have had support in the local twelve step community. I quickly noticed, however, that meetings were full of current and former clients. Even there I could not speak openly about what was going on in my life. This isolation played right into Frank's plans. I had nowhere else to turn.

My job contributed in a real way to what happened to me. I had no one with whom I could discuss the confusing aspects of my relationship, no one to give me a reality check. The situation at work continued to escalate. We were facing a review by an accreditation body, and the tensions started to rise. Ironically enough, I had been recruited by this accreditation company years before to become one of their surveyors. They employed people already working in the field to be part-time surveyors of similar programs in other geographical areas. In this way, the accreditation staff had firsthand working knowledge of the job. Employers were usually flattered to have one of their staff recruited, and my former employer had been happy to give me occasional time off to take trips to review other programs. I had thought that this qualification was one of the reasons Last Chance had hired me.

As the time for the accreditation review grew closer, I found out that my input was not wanted at all. They had their own ideas about how to prepare for the site survey. I could have saved them a lot of trouble, but I had learned by this time to keep my mouth shut. One day, things took a particularly unpleasant turn. We were all told that we would be working Saturday (for free) so that we could "tidy up" our files. I came to work as required, and we all gathered in a big room to work together.

I tidied up a bit but my files were already in good order. I saw, however, that my co-workers were busily rewriting theirs. They were basically fabricating a false record which was thought to be more in keeping with what the accreditation surveyors were looking for. Not only was what they were doing illegal and unethical, I knew that it was also unnecessary, and that the changes they were making would make no difference to the accreditation team. I grew increasingly uncomfortable with what was going on. I was not going to help my co-workers create fictional files, and so I quietly left the room and went home. I found out later that after I left, my coworkers were required to chant together: "Counselors are stupid, counselors are stupid." It was unbelievable.

This act of rebellion on my part brought things to a head. I knew I would be dragged over the coals at the earliest opportunity after the survey team had left. I told Frank what had happened, and he said: "You don't deserve to be treated that way. I know we are still getting to know each other. Maybe things will work out with us, and maybe they won't, but why don't you quit your job and move in with me in Garden City, and we will see if we can make this relationship work." I saw what looked to be the only possible way out of my employment dilemma; a way which would get me out of the job with my reputation and my hide still intact. On Monday, I went to work and told the owner of Last Chance that my boyfriend had asked me to move in with him. In other words, I told her that I wasn't leaving because there was anything wrong with her or her program, but rather because I had fallen in love. The ruse worked and after giving two weeks' notice, I left. They even gave me a cake and sang "For she's a jolly good fellow." I was the only counselor whom I saw leave on a good note in all the time I worked there, and we had a high staff turnover rate. When I left I had worked there just under ten months. I gave up my trailer and moved with my dog and two cats into Frank's townhouse in Garden City. I had successfully jumped from the frying pan into the fire.

Chapter Three

Walking into a trap

When I moved in with Frank, he told me to spread my things around and to make myself at home. However, we quickly encountered conflicts. It turned out he was very territorial, and God help me if I moved anything. Not only that, but he didn't want to give me any space of my own. Instead of giving me a drawer in a dresser, he gave me two half drawers. In this way, all of our stuff would be mixed together. I didn't really want to have to dig through his socks to find my bras, especially when he was so fussy about the way everything had to be. Shirts on hangers all had to be facing the same direction, with the buttons on the left or right accordingly. Socks and underwear had to be folded just so. He explained that he had attended a boarding school as a teenager, and they had shown him the "proper" way to do things. Simple things like leaving a dish cloth out to dry had to be done a certain way, and he would come around behind me and adjust things if I did it differently.

I rapidly realized I could do nothing right, and everything had to be his way. In addition to this, sleeping together every night became a huge source of stress for me. He suffered from insomnia, and I was a restless sleeper who rolled around a lot. He started a pattern of waking me up soon after I fell asleep because I would often move my legs in my sleep. It was like a form of torture, to be woken up repeatedly like that whenever I fell asleep. I suggested that I move to one of his kids' rooms when they were not there, but he insisted that we sleep together. Nights became anxiety-filled marathons as I lay there awake, trying not to move.

All these things made it bad enough that after three weeks of living together, I offered to move out. I had no job, nowhere to go, and I was living on savings. We had put my motorhome in storage, and I thought I could find somewhere in town to live in it, but he told me that people in Garden City didn't do that kind of thing. I found out many years later that this was one of the first big lies he told me. There were trailer parks in town as well as in neighboring districts. Some of them would have worked well for me, but I did not discover them. I took his word for it that there was nowhere for me to go, especially with a large dog and two cats. This made me feel trapped. Going back to Alaska would be a last resort. I tried hard to work things out. This is where I began to redraw my boundaries at my own expense in the interest of keeping the peace.

We gradually became used to living together as I continued to adjust my behaviour and my expectations. At this time, Frank encouraged me to take on another commitment. I had been told by a vet in First Landing that my old dog was sick and did not have long to live. Frank wanted to adopt a puppy. I had had a dog continuously for over twenty years by this time in my life, usually more than one, and I didn't really want to live without one. Since I was off work, I agreed that it would be a good time for me to raise a puppy, and it was not hard to convince me. This additional responsibility made me even more vulnerable, but I thought that if I could adjust enough, I could learn to get along with Frank. He was still very romantic with me sometimes when I behaved well, and he seemed to genuinely like my fur babies. I began to believe that the problems we had were things I could change. I was motivated to try to make this relationship work.

Frank was happy to explain to me the ways I didn't quite fit in, always with the view that he was just trying to help. Having returned to my native country after a long absence, I was anxious to be accepted. The constant campaign to change my toiletries, my underwear, and the way I dressed had expanded to my voice: its tone, volume, and phraseology. Words I spoke with an American accent, as well as phrases I used which he didn't like, were pointed out to me and corrected. While I was anxious to get rid of my American accent, so that I could fit in better, his corrections went beyond that. I felt like a country bumpkin who just didn't know how to blend in with polite society.

He said he was happy to help. He explained that it was not my fault that I didn't know better.

At first, his guidance seemed so benevolent. Yet it still had the desired effect of undermining my confidence. In addition to this, I was now trying to find a full-time job, and it was turning out to be much harder than I had expected. Garden City was a lovely place, and many people came from other parts of the country to live there. Competition for local jobs was fierce. I heard on a radio program at that time that the typical Garden City resident was a 45-year-old divorced woman working multiple part-time jobs. This described me exactly and was quite disconcerting. I did not feel I had the resources to move out on my own and provide for my animals. I was the type of person who would be willing to put up with a lot as long as my animals were happy, and they seemed to be. Many women become trapped in abusive relationships because of their children. My animals were equally dependent on me and just as important to me. I continued to bend to keep the peace.

There were many interests which Frank and I shared: a love of the outdoors, a love of animals, and a love for his youngest son, amongst others. These good things were the glue that kept our relationship going. The conflicts we had had when I first moved in gradually became less pronounced as I learned to do things his way, and we experienced a short time of relative peace and happiness. I was sleeping in another room about every third night, and I seemed to be able to get by with that amount of rest. He expected me to give this up as time passed, and I hoped that perhaps I could.

This is when Frank asked me to marry him. I felt very unsure about this idea, but I gave him a tentative yes. He was a package deal and I wanted the package, not realising at the time how tainted the package was. I had never had children of my own, and as I had grown older, this was one regret that I had started to have about my life. I found that I really enjoyed the parenting role I had been given with his young son. This connection surprised me. I had never wanted children before, and now I was surprised by my deepening bond with this young child. My maternal instincts had been awakened, and it was a strong lure. All I had to do was learn to be a little bit better person—or so I thought.

We set our wedding date for nine months after the proposal. I figured that by then I would be sure, and if not, I could call it off. I don't know if Frank knew I still had reservations, but putting our wedding so far into the future helped me give him that first, hesitant, yes. He was on his best behaviour and I could find little justi-fication for my doubts. He insisted that we had to be legally married to provide a good example for his chil-dren. Being somewhat old-fashioned myself, I could not argue with this reasoning. During our engagement, he started talking to me about us buying a house together. I had sold my house in Alaska by now and was looking to invest my money locally. I loved the area where we lived; it was everything I had been looking for in a more temperate climate. I was unsure about buying with him, but I realized my modest amount of capital was not adequate against the steep housing prices in the area. He started looking around and showing me what our pooled resources could buy. At one point, he actually got down on his knees and begged me to buy a house with him in the same district where his ex-wife lived. He wanted to have easier access to his children, where they could come and go without a car. She lived in a beautiful district on the outskirts of town, just the kind of place that suited my tastes perfectly. I found out years later that this was because she and I were very much alike.

I still had my doubts about becoming further entangled with this man, but at that time, we were by and large getting along. He was on his best behaviour, and I had a strong desire to put down roots. I thought our problems were mostly me. Perhaps I was somewhat damaged goods, as he implied, and should be grateful that he was willing to look past my imperfections and take me on. Perhaps I really was just a hick from Alaska, not quite fit for polite society.

I realize now that a woman with better self-esteem would never have fallen for his subtle manipulation. The insecurity I had always felt but tried to hide from the world was what made me perfect for him. Just like a predator can pick out the weakest animal from the herd, he had instinctively known I would be vulnerable to his constant, subtle, criticism. Instead of telling him to take a hike I gave in, I tried to adapt. My indoctrination was well underway.

Frank started actively looking for property near his ex-wife. When he found a really nice one, he took me to look at it. I only looked at a couple of places before we found "the one." It was a house which spoke to me the moment I walked into it. I remember thinking that

I would be willing to do a lot for the possibility of living there. It had a large, private, fenced back yard that would be perfect for my two dogs and two cats. It had a beautiful back deck where I could imagine sitting and drinking a cup of tea in the morning. Just like my affection for his son, me who had never before imagined the possibility of motherhood, this house was nicer than any place I had ever imagined I could live.

Frank put together the deal with the banks and the real estate agents. By combining our resources, we could make a large down payment, which would make the house just barely affordable for us. I was still unsure about our relationship, even though we were getting along at that time. He was doing everything he could to charm me. To further tempt me, the house had two separate living areas, upstairs and downstairs. I foolishly thought we could live together as roommates if the relationship didn't work out, with one of us upstairs and one of us downstairs. Nevertheless, there was always an anxious feeling in the pit of my stomach when I considered these commitments, but I didn't trust myself enough, I didn't have enough faith in myself to listen. Something in my gut was trying to warn me that I was walking into a trap, but I ignored my intuition and kept going.

We bought the house in April and moved right in. We were scheduled to be married in July, and still I wasn't sure if I should go through with the marriage or not. There were increased conflicts when we moved in, but Frank attributed this to the stress of moving, and I believed him. The feeling in my stomach, however, would not go away. About a month before our wedding date, we went on a kayak camping trip. Our relationship always worked best when we were camping. It was an idyllic trip with perfect weather, in a spectacularly beautiful country, and we had a good time. He was much less bossy with me when we were camping. We came back to town and I thought: "Well, I already own a house with the man; I might as well marry him." So I followed through with the wedding plans, and walked right into hell.

Chapter Four

The marriage

I have read stories in books about domestic violence describing how the first time the woman was assaulted was at her own wedding reception. My situation was not that different, although Frank never hit me. Our marriage precipitated a significant and permanent change in our relationship; the abuse intensified exponentially.

I wonder what it is that makes a man turn on the woman he has just married. I doubt if I will ever really understand what happened. The whole situation was and still is incomprehensible to me. What I do know is that things between us changed abruptly as soon as we were married. He begged me to move in with him, buy a house with him, and marry him. After I had done all that, I suddenly became public enemy number one. I did not say or do anything on our honeymoon to cause this change. We did not talk that much on our honeymoon. All we did was play various sex games which he had devised. We had gone to a nearby resort for five days, and when I questioned how quiet and withdrawn he had become he blamed his behaviour on exhaustion from all the wedding planning.

It was something more than that though. I took a picture of him sitting in the private hot tub that went with our cabin, and the look he gave me through the camera lens was practically malevolent. It confused me. We came back to town on the sixth day and sometime on the seventh day, exactly one week after our wedding, he said to me: "I hate my life, you better figure out how to divorce me." I could not have been more stunned.

It is hard to explain the way I felt at this time: confused, hurt, betrayed, bewildered and embarrassed. I didn't know where to turn. How could I admit that the marriage so carefully planned had already hit the wall in just one week? It was too humiliating for words. I felt like a fool and an utter failure. I didn't understand how someone who had pursued me steadily for two years, begging me to blend my life with his, could have changed his mind so quickly? We had not had a fight. What had caused this abrupt change? How could I understand it? How could I explain it to my friends and to the family who had traveled from Alaska to celebrate with us? I was too ashamed and confused to say anything to anyone, and so my isolation truly began.

Things continued to be terrible between us as we settled into life in our new house as newlyweds. Frank kept going into rages over the smallest detail. He started to call me terrible names. The longer we stayed together the viler the names became. Over the years, my husband called me

Cunt, Bitch, Whore, Slob, Hick, Shit Hole of a Wife, and a Curse from God. These names were always designed to hit me in whatever spot he thought was most vulnerable at the time. These names were reserved for me when no one else was listening. They became part of my private hell.

Frank started to say that he hated our house and wanted to sell it. Frank was the kind of man who always wanted something he didn't have. He would buy cars, after spending a long time researching them, only to quickly want to trade them in on something else right after he assumed ownership. After he sold several cars out from under me, I finally convinced him to let me have a car just in my name. I used the excuse of needing to establish my own credit history in Canada. In this way, I was finally able to hold on to a car for more than six months.

As for the house, I did not want to sell the place we had just purchased. I had finally found somewhere that felt like home to me. I never wanted to move again, yet I was still only working multiple part-time jobs. I had no financial security and was terrified I would not be able to find housing for myself and my animals without Frank. I worked harder and found more jobs, but full-time employment still eluded me. It was difficult, but I began to see work as a refuge, and since our financial circumstances were very tight, he never complained about me working. It got to the point where I was working seven part-time jobs with five different employers. Several of the jobs were on-call shift work. I would work shifts back to back, often sixteen hours at a stretch, frequently overnight. I was going to work at 3:00pm and getting off work at 7:00am. It was exhausting, but it was easier than being at home.

Frank's mood grew increasingly unpredictable. It would have been easier if he had always been nasty to me, but he would follow a particularly bad stretch by suddenly being attentive and kind to me. While he wouldn't normally apologize for his behaviour, temper, or his unreasonable outbursts, he would explain them away by saying he had had a headache, or he had been tired. The pendulum swung back and forth between love and affection then rejection and hostility. It left me reeling in confusion and despair. He would usually blame his outbursts on something I had done. I had talked too much, I had been too loud, or maybe I had moved something I shouldn't have. I began to walk on eggshells, trying to avoid provoking his anger.

To further add to the stress in my life, he had started calling in sick to work as soon as we returned from our honeymoon. He had a stable job as an office worker, and while we were courting, he told me that he planned to retire later rather than early because of the time he had missed after his car accident. Now, all of a sudden, he began to miss a lot of work. I began to dread coming home from a night shift at 7:30 in the morning only to see his car still in the driveway; it meant he had called in sick again. I was working as many hours as I could, but I still could not protect us from losing our home if he lost his job. My anxiety increased. He began to have meetings with his employer and his union representative about his attendance. What I didn't know when I married him was that Frank was already failing at work long before I met him. He hid this from me. His employer had even done some psychometric testing on him to see how they could accommodate him at work, to help him be successful and stay employed. He had some specific skill deficits, but his problems were mostly associated with his personality and his way of relating to people, specifically women.

When Frank came to stay with me in First Landing, before we were married, he always insisted on spending Sunday night with me, getting up early to drive home Monday morning. What I didn't know was that he usually called in sick on these Mondays, going home and slipping back into bed. Instead of being honest with me about his limitations, he pretended to be much healthier, much stronger, much more successful, and much more financially secure than he was. Whenever I went to his place I always went home Sunday night. I wanted to get a good night's sleep and prepare for work Monday morning. He always made me feel guilty for this, as if there was something wrong with me for going home. He knew I wanted to avoid that one-and-a-half-hour drive first thing in the morning. He complained that I didn't care as much about the relationship as he did.

Frank began complaining of headaches and fatigue and went to multiple doctors looking for a solution. After his car accident, he had suffered from chronic headaches and insomnia, for which he took medication. He had been off work for a while after his accident, but when I met him he was back at work full-time, and I believed he would just continue to get better and better. However, Frank's absenteeism at work increased rapidly after our marriage, and he eventually wound up on short-term disability. This meant that he received about three-quarters of his former income. Now we were in real financial trouble. The house had been a stretch for us financially, and I was beginning to realize that Frank had a spending problem. He would skip lunch rather than bring a sandwich to work, but then kept himself going with three or four designer coffees. He would also buy things we didn't need because he could get Air Miles points from the purchase. There was no logic to it but I couldn't stop him.

The pendulum continued to swing back and forth. Sometimes he was incredibly cruel to me, and then, just when I might have given up and walked out, he would pull me back in with affection and tenderness. It was like being married to the fictional character Dr. Jekyll and Mr. Hyde. My new husband was sometimes attentive and nice, only to be some kind of monster during other times.

Due to our increasing financial difficulties, I took on even more shifts. My work became even more of a refuge for me. I was working with people who had alcohol and drug problems, as well as people with severe mental illness. I found working with these intoxicated and/or psychotic people easier to handle than my home life, which says a lot. Meanwhile, Frank began to seek out more assistance from doctors and support agencies. He was always trying to find something or someone else to make him happy. By then, I knew that I was not the one who could do it. At one point, he had a support worker from the brain injury program come over to help him sort out closets. This seemed strange to me because I could have easily helped him. However, since I had become public enemy number one, everything I said was suspect.

It frequently seemed like he hated me. I just stayed out of it, therefore, and let him do what he wanted. I have since learned that I am easily controlled by someone else's rage. I will twist myself into a pretzel trying to avoid further provoking an angry person. I am not sure why I am this way. I just had no experience in how to handle the frequent outbursts directed at me. I continued to try and placate him, doing anything to avoid provoking his rage. I realize now this made the situation worse.

There were times when no matter how hard I tried, I could not stay out of the line of fire. His eldest son had started avoiding our home, but his youngest, Tommy, was often stuck in the middle of our nightmare because of a forced visitation schedule. I loved Tommy and did everything I could to shelter him. Frank definitely kept his worst behavior for when Tommy was not around, but he still saw some of our bad days. Frank could turn his rage on and off depending on who was around. My mentally ill clients could not turn their madness on and off like that. When they were having a bad episode, it happened no matter who was around. Frank, however, always had a level of control over his acting out. I eventually became convinced that his behaviour had more to do with bullying and dominating me than anything else, but it took me years to come to this conclusion, and to have enough compassion for myself to find a way to escape.

One of the worst episodes occurred six months into our marriage. The three of us—Frank, Tommy, and myself—had gone for a walk with the dogs in a local park. I have no idea what set Frank off that day, but he became furious. We stopped at a grocery store on the way home and I quickly went inside to buy a few items so that I could cook dinner. By the time I got back to the car, he was even more furious, over what, I don't know. When we stopped for gas at a station near our house, he jumped out of the car and started walking home. Poor Tommy also got out and began to follow his father, not knowing what else to do, I suppose. I drove home and when they got there shortly afterward, Frank sent Tommy back to his mother's house. Now I was alone with a monster.

He stormed around the house, going up and down the stairs, while I sat quietly in the living room, shaking. I was terrified of his unexplained rage. A couple of times I asked him what was wrong but he wouldn't speak to me. This went on for some time, and I gradually realized that he was packing. I asked him a couple of times if he was going somewhere, but he didn't answer me. He was a tall man, a full eight inches taller than I was, and he seemed to be in a complete rage for some unknown reason. I had never been more afraid of him.

Finally, he left the house and drove away. I decided that I had to get out, and I began throwing a few things together into my own car. My dogs had been outside all of this time; I always tried to keep them away from him when he was angry. I put them in my car and got ready to leave, though I had no idea where I would go. When I went to get my sleeping bag, however, I discovered that he had dug out my shotgun from storage and taken it with him. Since we had children in the house, my shotgun had been hidden deep in a closet under the stairs. A person had to crawl in to get it out. I looked and found he had also taken the ammunition, which had been locked up in a different location. Now I was really worried. I quickly left the house and drove to a side street in our neighborhood where I parked out of sight. I didn't know what to do. I took out my cell phone and called one of his best friends, who also happened to work at the brain injury support program, but she didn't answer. I then called the man who had been his best friend since childhood, who also volunteered with people with disabilities; again, no answer.

As I thought about the gun and wondered what he meant to do with it, I became convinced that I had no choice but to call the police. It did not occur to me that he was going to shoot me, but I became worried that he might hurt himself. I thought of his children and realized I had to do something. If he killed himself and I had done nothing to try and stop him, I could never forgive myself. So I called the police and told them my situation. I told them I was afraid he meant to commit suicide. The police, however, had a very different idea. They believed he was thinking of hurting me, and they told me to stay out of sight. While I was talking to them on the phone, I saw his car pass by on the street in front of me, headed back to our house. They told me to stay put, and they showed up with a couple of police cars. They arrested him and took him to the emergency psychiatric ward at the hospital. I went back to the house and an officer came and spoke to me. He looked around and saw that among the photographs in frames displayed around the house, the ones with me in them had all been placed face down. Frank had started to do this whenever he was mad at me. The officer spoke to me with concern about my safety. I told him I had had enough and would end the marriage, so he left. After about an hour and a half I got a phone call from this officer. He told me that Frank was being released from the hospital and was on his way home. I grabbed a few things and fled with my dogs.

I checked into a hotel in town, careful to park my car out of sight, and stayed there a couple of days. At first I kept my cell phone off because I was feeling so exhausted and overwhelmed, but I eventually turned it on. I began receiving messages from Frank. The police had confiscated the shotgun, but Frank had convinced the psychiatrist that it was all a big misunderstanding. I don't know how much information the officers had given to the hospital, but true to form, Frank was able to change his behaviour in front of witnesses and spin a story that others believed. He said he had just been going camping, and his wife had overreacted because she was unstable due to a mental health problem. They believed him.

I was asked by the police to come in and make a state-ment, which I did. Frank's voice messages were at first mainly focused on forbidding me from talking to the police, but my compliant nature meant I wasn't going to ignore a direct request from the police. I am sure my statement to them sounded very disjointed. How could I explain to them what was going on, when I didn't know myself? The months of chaos, fear, and overwork had taken a toll on me, and I was completely overwhelmed and baffled by my situation. I really have no idea what I told them. I gave my statement and Frank was finally charged with transporting a firearm in an unsafe condition. There was no mention of domestic violence.

The hotel was expensive and I knew I couldn't stay there for long. Frank's phone messages eventually became more conciliatory, saying I had overreacted to him having a bad day. After a couple of days, I eventually spoke to him on the phone and he begged me to come back home. I didn't know what else to do. I had limited resources and two large dogs that needed their back yard. I didn't have any close friends I could talk to about this mess, and I was too embarrassed to tell my family. Like so many women in my situation, I was isolated, embarrassed, confused, and broke.

When I finally came home, Frank got down on his knees and begged me to give him another chance. He told me he loved me and that I was the best thing that had ever happened to him. He said he would be completely lost without me. After the six months of hostility following our marriage, this was like soothing rain on the parched desert of my heart. I wanted to believe him. I thought maybe the crisis was finally over and he would see me again as his friend. I decided to give us another try.

We never really talked about what had happened that night, which was also typical of our relationship. When the storms had passed, I was always so relieved and exhausted that I often did not want to rock the boat by bringing things up. This behaviour is quite contrary to my nature. I usually want to talk about things, work them out, and come to an understanding. The fact that I often gave up on trying to do this with Frank tells me how far my loss of self had progressed by this point. Instead I began to secretly look for other housing options, but I couldn't find anything. The housing market in our area was particularly tight and expensive. People call it a "sunshine tax" for living somewhere beautiful. To me it was a gilded cage. We had sold my motorhome to help with the down payment on our house. I had put all of my eggs in one basket, and now I needed to try and keep the peace until I could figure out what to do.

This pattern repeated itself over and over again throughout our marriage. Frank would act in an outrageous fashion whenever there were no witnesses around, but he would pull it together in front of others including doctors, police, his friends, and the general public. He would be absolutely charming to the clerk at the grocery store, only to rip my head off as soon as we got in the car. He blamed all of his problems on his brain injury, but he had control of his behaviour in front of others. This did not match what I knew about people with brain injuries, but it is typical in situations of domestic violence. He was very adept at knowing just how to control me, just what threats would have the greatest impact. Once, when I had left the house to escape one of Frank's verbal assaults, he called me on my cell phone and threatened to put our two dogs in the street—where they could easily be hit by one of the many cars that drove by—if I did not come back home immediately. Needless to say, I complied. No one else who knew him would ever have believed he would do such a thing.

By now feeling afraid, overwhelmed, and bewildered was my normal state of existence. There were so many small incidents, which, added together, kept me completely off balance. Some of these incidents happened despite my best efforts to avoid upsetting Frank, as he would change the rules in the middle of the game. After being on short-term disability for a while Frank tried to go back to work part-time. He was still living on expensive lattes and had become a frequent customer of the coffee shop in his building. He was always charming to the staff there, and they thought he was a really nice guy. One day, they gave him one of their coffee mugs with the store logo on it. The mug was red, and when he proudly brought it home, he explained to me that this was his mug, and I was not to use it. We had another one of their mugs in blue already, and he told me I could use that one. I was careful to follow his instructions. A few weeks later, he saw that I was using the blue mug. He said to me: "No, no, no, no. You are only supposed to use the red one. Remember, red is for girls, blue is for boys." Even though I knew this was a direct contradiction of his previous instructions, I just apologized and switched mugs. By now I would do almost anything to avoid upsetting him. Keeping the peace had become my top priority. Nevertheless, the constant changing of the rules kept me continually off balance.

Following the incident with the gun Frank hired a lawyer to get all charges against him dropped. I had to go to these lawyer appointments and I was made out to be the crazy wife who constantly overreacted to the smallest thing. It was humiliating, but there was no way I was going to contradict him. The lawyer was able to negotiate a deal so that as long as there were no further incidents for five years, all record of this offense would be dropped. I was instructed to never speak to the police again.

In between these confusing times, there were short periods of calm. Frank would suddenly become playful and attentive, and I would get a glimmer of the man I had thought I was marrying. I realize now that this is the part that other people never understand. If he had been continually awful to me, it would have been so much easier to make the decision to flee, no matter the consequences. But he had an instinct for just how far he could push me, just how much I would take. When I reached this limit, he would suddenly switch, flattering me with love and praise, doing little considerate things for me. It made me doubt my perceptions. How could he be so considerate if he was such a monster? Maybe I was over-reacting; maybe it wasn't such a big deal. I didn't know the truth, and because I was emotionally isolated and the bad behaviour never happened in front of witnesses, I had no one to validate my reality and tell me I wasn't crazy. Our relationship seemed to bounce continually between heaven and hell.

The hardest part was never knowing which aspect of Frank I would be dealing with at any given time. Sometimes, when I needed him the most, he would refuse to help me, even if, when others needed him in the same situation, he would totally step up to the plate. We lived in an area where snow was rare, so when it did fall, the streets were particularly dangerous. The area had very little snow removal equipment and many streets were built with sharp angles and inclines of a type which would be avoided in snow country. One night, when I was driving home from work at 11:30pm, six inches of snow had accumulated on the highway and my car wasn't really equipped for it. To get home I had to make a sharp left turn off the highway, and then follow a steep, curving incline. I did not believe my car could make it in the snow, but I tried anyway, and wound up sliding backward until I was horizontal across the oncoming lane of traffic. I was able to turn around and get back on the highway. I had to travel several miles in the wrong direction before I could find a place to turn around and head towards home again. I ran through intersections and red lights because I feared that if I stopped, I would get stuck. Fortunately, there were almost no other cars on the road. I called home, hoping to get Frank's advice on taking a different path home, avoiding the big hill. Tommy answered; I told him it was an emergency and that I needed him to wake up his dad, which he did.

Frank came on the line, and I tried to explain my situation to him, asking for an alternate route home. I was talking very fast, the stress of the drive catching up with me. Frank interrupted to say he didn't like my tone of voice and then hung up on me. I was flabbergasted. Frank had a reputation among his acquaintances and family of being very safety conscious, of being good at first aid, and being prepared for emergencies. He loved to consider himself the person others could turn to in a crisis. When he would say "Trust me," he expected others to give up any doubts and blindly step off any ledge he indicated. One of his complaints about me was that I did not display the expected level of blind trust. Despite this reputation, the reality was that asking for help was not an option; with no witnesses around, I was dealing with a different Frank. I eventually made it home and crawled into bed, feeling alone and exhausted. I began to think that if I was drowning, and needed Frank to throw me a rope, he was much more likely to stand on the shore and lecture me about the poor choices which had led to my problem, rather than offer any aid. He wouldn't throw the rope. I was on my own.

Chapter Five

Trying to make it work

Despite all these difficulties, there were still things which kept us together. We shared a love of camping and kayaking, and often these trips away were the glue upon which our relationship depended. In addition to this, I had loved Frank when I married him and been full of hope that I could have a family. It took a while for my heart to let go. I kept thinking that I could figure out a way to solve our problems and save our marriage. Sometimes, when things were good between us, he even apologized in a general way for things that had happened between us. He blamed our difficulties on his brain injury and on my not responding to his needs appropriately.

We saw the first of several counselors. He and I met with her separately at first, and after listening to my side of the story, she told me it sounded like a classic pattern of domestic violence. After talking with Frank, however, she told us together that she was confused and she didn't know what the problem was. He could be very convincing, and I realized he had successfully manipulated her and that she couldn't help me. I agreed to terminate this first attempt at counseling. I couldn't afford it anyway.

Frank's attempt to go back to work was short lived, and he switched from short-term to long-term disability. He blamed his inability to work on stress at home, and so we were assigned a counselor who specialized in working with people with brain injuries. Frank believed that if I could just learn to become more supportive, understanding, and accommodating, then all of our problems would be solved. The counselor tried to work with us, but we seemed to have different agendas. I was already being as flexible and supportive as was humanly possible, but Frank did not tell the story that way. Since this counselor was being paid for by the brain injury program, the focus was on me learning to support Frank's needs. This perfectly supported and enabled Frank's violence towards me. In the few brief moments when I was alone with this counselor, he told me to get out of my marriage, saying it was never going to get better. This was not what I wanted to hear at the time, and further confused me. When we saw the counselor together he focused on Frank's needs, and we discussed how I could be more supportive. In addition to these conflicting messages, the counselor seemed to be afraid of Frank.

During one session, the hopelessness of my situation really hit me, and when the session ended I left in tears. I walked out of the office and into a park next door, where I sat down on the grass with my back against a tree, crying. Frank came up to me and violently smashed his water bottle on the trunk of the tree, inches above my head. The message was clear: if I didn't stop crying, I was going to get hurt. In our following counseling session, I tried to talk about this incident. I wanted the counselor to know the kind of violence I was living with. Frank denied that there was any covert threat in his actions. He explained that he had just been frustrated, and he hit his water bottle against the tree to vent his frustration, and this just happened to be the only tree around. While this was certainly not true, the conversation moved on in a different direction; my attempt to address the violence was lost. I tried to come back to how intimidated and afraid I often felt, trying to explain that our problems were not just a result of my "lack of understanding." After a period of getting nowhere, I gave up. One more failed attempt at counseling.

Since the brain injury program was paying for our sessions, I suppose the counselor had to take the approach of helping me understand and adjust my behaviour to support Frank's brain injury. This made the domestic violence worse. The last thing an abusive man needs is a counselor supporting his notion that it is primarily the woman who needs to change. The only time this counselor supported me was when he suggested to me privately that I get out of the relationship. Based on this experience, I would warn any woman who tries to enter counselling with an abusive man to make sure that the counselor understands the issues, or else there is a very real possibility that the counseling will make the problem worse.

The housing situation in our town combined with my financial circumstances kept me feeling trapped. Frank had a real spending problem, and we had to refinance our house a couple of times in the first two years to pay off his credit card debt, but he would just rack it up again right afterward. He bought things we neither needed nor could afford. He bought cans of paint because he said we needed to repaint the house, but his real motivation was, yet again, to accumulate Air Miles points. It made no logical sense, since he never actually put the paint on the house, and I certainly did not have time to do so. When Frank and I finally divorced, I threw out about fifteen cans of paint which had been sitting outside for all those years. It seemed like I was always trying to compensate for a flood of expenditures. Despite my willingness to work hard, I was outmatched by his compulsive spending. Frank always bought top-of-the-line items no matter what he purchased, justifying the extra expenditure by declaring the item could be passed on to his children later, whether he was buying garden shears or camping equipment. He was a classic example of someone who has champagne taste on a beer budget. The fact that I just had to pick up more shifts to try and keep us in the black didn't seem to bother him at all. Any attempt to speak to Frank about his spending led to a fight. He really believed he was being reasonable. Frank had grown up very wealthy and he had a strong sense of entitlement. He expected the best of everything and had no real concept of how everyday people economized. His basic selfishness pervaded every-thing, and my needs were irrelevant and a nuisance to him.

About two years into our marriage, I finally got a full -time position, and I quit several of my part-time jobs. In my new job, I worked at a residential facility for people with chronic and severe mental illness. I still took one or two extra shifts per week working with people who suffered from chemical dependency, mostly working at a shelter for the homeless community. I also did one four-hour shift per week at the local prison, screening new inmates for suicide risk. Compared to each of these three jobs, I found my relationship with Frank to be the most difficult thing I did, but who could I tell who would understand what I was going through? I still had no one. I made some friends in my various jobs, but I really had no time to socialize. With the few people I did try to confide in I discovered that people don't really want to hear about this type of domestic violence. People just seemed to blame me for being in this situation. I looked for support and help, but I could not find it. With most of my co-workers it was just too embarrassing to discuss. I felt that they would only think less of me if they knew.

Our relationship continued to be turbulent, with good days mixed with very bad ones. I was grateful for my full-time job, which gave my life some structure and stability. Meanwhile, Frank had failed at work completely. He was on long term disability, applying for permanent disability. This meant that there was no relief in sight from our financial difficulties. I was desperate to hold on to my home. My dogs and cats seemed happy and I was really enjoying Tommy's visits. It seemed at the time that there was more benefit to us staying together than splitting up. I also thought that when the stress of trying to work was removed, perhaps Frank and I would get along better. I didn't realize the toll our relationship was taking on me. The chaos had come to feel almost normal. My boundaries had slipped so far that I no longer recognized how much of myself I had lost.

The brain injury program found us yet another counselor. This time things seemed different. He was very expensive and very good. I felt that he had a better understanding of what was going on. Most importantly, he was neither afraid of nor intimidated by Frank. He actually confronted Frank a few times during our sessions about his rage and his unrealistic expectation that others cater to him. This did not go over well, but it sure was a relief to me. We started to address things that had never been addressed before, such as Frank's bullying of his youngest son. Once, I even found the courage to make a reference to his alcohol consumption and how this was not a good mix with all the medication he was taking. He stormed out of that session. I realized then that our issues would never really be discussed; Frank was not willing to participate in an open dialogue.

Frank's program only paid for six sessions with that counselor and we could not afford to continue on our own. I was sad because I had hoped that this counselor might have been able to help me, and if nothing else, it was nice not to be blamed for everything. Nevertheless, we needed to focus our energies on other things. Frank was facing a trying process of applying for permanent disability. The final step consisted of him being interviewed by a psychiatrist who would make the ultimate determination on his ability to work. After an extended period of paperwork and doctor visits, his application for permanent disability was approved. It was interesting to me that, in his report, the psychiatrist stated that Frank's brain injury was exacerbated by pre-existing, underlying personality issues, which started in his family of origin. He said that together, these made Frank unable to work. In other words, he was not a previously healthy man with a brain injury; he was a man with significant issues aggravated by the injury, which led to his disability. This matched what I had come to believe myself. It was why everyone found the situation so confusing. He did not fit any particular stereotype. Yes, he had a mild brain injury, but that did not explain his behaviour, or the difficulties I encountered trying to be his wife.

Frank attributed all of his problems to stress, and he told everyone that I was his main stressor. He was happy to believe that if I was somehow different, things would be easier for us. This fed the pattern of domestic violence, and was very destructive to me. He said that if I could just speak differently, or act differently, or move differently, or be different, everything would be so much better. By now, I had lost so much of myself that I began to try, if only to keep the peace. His attempts to completely control my behaviour increased. For example, he developed a hand signal which he used to silently communicate to me that I should speak more quietly, or less, or not at all, when other people were around. He treated me like a radio he could turn on or off. I felt like a puppet on a string, constantly under his control. When we were in public, we kept up the facade of a functioning couple. People would have been shocked if they had known the extent to which things had progressed behind closed doors. Getting permanent disability was supposed to be the Holy Grail that would solve all our problems. This was another promise which did not turn out to be true. Once he was off work and had a guaranteed, very respectable, income, nothing changed. He was still hostile, and I was still the problem.

I lived on a precipice, sometimes falling into despair, and sometimes being recaptured by glimmers of hope. He knew just how far he could push me before he needed to reel me back in again with kindness. I did not want to get a divorce. I wanted to be a part of Tommy's life; I wanted to have a family, to be a mother, to have a home, to have a husband to share my life with. When he chose to be nice to me, it gave me hope and prolonged my agony.

Other issues kept me isolated and confused. After three or four years of marriage, I discovered what had motivated Frank's earlier gifts of lingerie when we were dating: he had a fetish for women's underwear and lingerie. He liked to shop for it, he liked to handle it, and he particularly liked to wear it. It turned out his gifts to me were really gifts to himself, but he hid this from me for several years, until we were married and I was well and truly entangled. Then I found out that he wanted me to make love with him while he was wearing these woman's undergarments, and I just couldn't; it was too much of a turn off. He didn't let me know about these proclivities until our situation was such that it would be very hard for me to get away. What had looked on the surface like generosity when he was giving me these gifts was actually very selfish.

Frank's fetish for women's lingerie turned out to be just the tip of the iceberg. The longer we were together, the more I discovered hidden aspects of the man I had married. By nature, I am a fairly open-minded person, and I could have accepted Frank's desire to wear women's underwear as long as he didn't want me to participate in the experience. Unfortunately, Frank's inherent selfishness meant that he had little regard for my feelings, especially if they got in the way of what he wanted to do.

About four years after our wedding, my mother paid for us to take a vacation to Hawaii. She knew we had been under a lot of stress for a long time, but I had not admitted to her the level of abuse I was experiencing because I felt so ashamed. We accepted her gift and went on a two-week holiday. What I didn't anticipate was that once we were away from home, Frank started cross dressing in public. He wore long sarongs around his waist, which looked just like a skirt; he wore dangle earrings, rings, bracelets, toe rings, and ankle bracelets. He wore nail polish and eye make-up, including mascara. He came completely out of the closet and he began to turn the heads of people everywhere we went. Surprisingly, many men looked at him appreciatively when he walked by. It was humiliating for me to walk into a coffee shop or a restaurant and have half the men there swivel their heads to look at my husband, many with admiring glances. Gay men started making passes at him and exchanging signals with him everywhere we went. He would leave my side to use the washroom and would be propositioned as soon as he was 10 feet away from me. It was obvious we were a married couple, so this put me in the embarrassing position of being "the wife who doesn't know" in the eyes of others. Frank seemed to really enjoy the attention he was getting, and being with me he felt safe while he indulged his fetish. I have no problem with transvestite men, but I didn't really want to date one, nor did

I want to take on the role of the wife of a man dressed as a woman. One evening, when we were walking down the sidewalk, a Christian missionary actually stopped us and offered to pray for us on the spot. Frank was having too much fun to notice or care about my feelings or my embarrassment over being forced to participate in the spectacle he was making of himself.

I didn't know how to handle Frank dressing in drag for our whole vacation. I tried talking to him about it, asking him to tone it down, but my protests fell on deaf ears. I guess all I could have done was to get on an airplane and fly back home. One lasting impact on me was that I stopped wearing makeup. I didn't want to be in the unenviable position of being in competition with my husband over who was the prettiest. He was a good-looking man, tall, slender, with big blue eyes. I was stunned to find out how many men were interested in my husband. Even some waiters went crazy over him, flirting with him when we went out to dinner. When we went to the beach, he was often propositioned as soon as he left my side. He could have easily had sex in the washroom at almost every beach we went to. Fortunately for me he didn't want to act on these offers, at least not that I know of, but he sure liked the attention, and telling me about it afterwards. I didn't know what to do except to pretend I didn't notice or I didn't care. The truth was that I felt humiliated and resented being forced to play the role of the fool. When we left Hawaii, he said he real-ized that I had probably had a miserable time. He guessed I wouldn't ever want to go back. This was definitely how

I felt. Knowing how I felt, however, did not seem to have any impact on his behaviour.

Frank often used me as a shield to deflect taking responsibility for what he wanted to do and from admitting who he really was. Sometime before our trip, and several years after we were married, Frank had had his nipples pierced. This was something he pressured me to do as well, but I steadfastly refused. The war over the treatment of my nipples was a sore point (pun intended) between us for most of our relationship. Frank was projecting his desires onto me. When Frank's very conservative friends noticed later that he was wearing nipple rings, he blamed me, telling them mysteriously that he had lost a bet with me. I have no idea what his conservative, childhood friends thought of me, I just know that their opinion was based on lies.

This pattern of telling lies to his friends about me was ongoing. Frank sometimes acted violently when we were at home, putting holes in walls and doors, but he always had a glib explanation for the damage he caused. He usually patched holes fairly quickly and went through great efforts to find matching paint to cover them. I would listen with amazement at his easy explanation to friends if they asked about it. He would describe tripping over something I had left on the floor, or some other such nonsense. I am not sure what his friends thought of these explanations. He sounded pretty convincing, but I had been there when the hole was made, and I always experienced this type of violent acting out as a covert threat, showing me just what kind of damage he could do if he chose to. Once he put a hole in a wall when I had a client downstairs in my office. I had tried to run an addiction recovery aftercare program out of my home after we were married, but this business venture was short-lived because I could not count on Frank to keep his behaviour together when I had clients in the house. Having someone punching holes in walls while I had a client downstairs was awkward, to say the least.

Frank was violent in other ways as well. On one occasion, Frank destroyed the stove upstairs while Tommy and I were downstairs watching TV. By the time this happened, both Tommy and I knew better than to go upstairs when things got noisy. The stove was replaced the next day and the old one hauled away. We never spoke about these incidents. I was just expected to live with his violent outbursts.

I believe that the number one reason Frank never actually hit me was because this would have decisively put him in the category of an abusive man. Frank cared too much about his perception of himself as a nice guy. He cared very much about other people perceiving him this way, too. Everything he did to me had to be hidden or deniable. If he had left a bruise on me, others would have known. The bruises to my spirit and my heart were invisible, and he therefore did not care about them. He could still maintain his illusion of being a good guy and a gentleman.

Frank went even further than just making excuses for holes in walls and doors. He often directly accused me of whatever he was doing. For example, if he was yelling at me, or being sarcastic, he would accuse me of yelling or being sarcastic. If he was spending money recklessly, he would accuse me of doing so. He would walk all over my boundaries and then accuse me of doing the same. This kept me on the defensive. Often I would make the mistake of trying to explain or prove that I was not doing what he accused me of. It turned out to be a very effective way of preventing me from addressing issues or bringing things up. I was too busy defending myself. It was so confusing, and it sure made our counselors' heads spin; they didn't know who to believe, and I don't blame them. He was a master manipulator, and I was no match for him.

Towards the end of our relationship, after about six or seven years, I realized that the best way for me to know what Frank was up to was to listen to what he accused me of doing. If he was talking about me behind my back, he would accuse me of doing this. If he was being manipulative and secretive, he would accuse me of the same. Once I came to understand this bait and switch tactic, it helped me to figure things out. I wonder how much he really believed of all the things he said. His ability to manipulate others, including me, was incredible.

Walking all over my boundaries was a daily occurrence. He would decide that he did not like some piece of my clothing, and so he would hide it from me, and if I did not ask for it quickly enough, he would throw it out, explaining later if I asked that he thought I didn't want it anymore. He would go behind me and rearrange things that were exclusively mine. He would go into my gym bag and take out the shampoo or other items to "clean" my bag, and I would not discover this until I found myself without what I needed at the gym. By now, we were sleeping in separate bedrooms, and another thing he liked to do was to go into my room and switch the duvet cover around. I liked to keep the buttons at the foot of the bed so that my long hair did not get tangled in them while I slept, but he would persistently switch this when I was not looking. He explained that the duvet cover would wear better if it was rotated in this way. So then, when I came home after working a night shift, dead on my feet, I would have to remake my bed before I could get into it. No matter how many times I asked him to stop doing these kinds of things, he refused; he believed his way was better than mine.

Sometimes these invasions even followed me to work. One day, Frank stopped by my new place of employment. He went into the washroom and saw that we had a can of air freshener in there. He came out and scolded me about it, saying we should not be using such a product, which he considered harmful to one's health, and then he threw it in the garbage. I waited until he had left, then dug the air freshener out of the garbage and put it back. It was useless to explain to him that I shared the office with others, and throwing out this item was neither his nor my decision to make.

After we had agreed to divorce but were still living in the same house, I put a deadbolt on my bedroom door and kept it locked all the time. I was so sick of trying to keep track of my things when they were being moved, rearranged, and disposed of behind my back. I wanted to know that my possessions would still be there, and not changed, when I got home. Just before he moved out, he actually had this door unlocked while I was out of town and went through my things one last time. I know this because he took a small sea shell I had found in Hawaii which I kept on a shelf in my room. I am sure he thought I was hiding valuable, secret assets in my bedroom, which is why he had a locksmith open the door while I was out of town visiting my mother. He did not realize just how much it had come to mean to me to be able to turn my back and have my stuff be left alone. After he moved out, I found my seashell in a suitcase he had packed and left behind. I was amazed that he could stoop to take such a small item, which had no monetary value and was only significant to me. But that was the kind of thing he had been doing on a regular basis for years. I put the deadbolt on my door because I just could not stand it anymore.

There were other ways that Frank tried to control every corner of my life. When I first moved to Garden City, Frank arranged it so that he and I had the same physician. This seemed like a favour to me, because physicians were in short supply. Unfortunately, he later accused me of taking a bottle of his pills to cover up his own medication abuse. He was going through them much too quickly. Later when I finally broke down in my doctor's office and told her about some of the abuse I was experiencing, I found out that her mind was already made up against me, and I was stunned by her judgemental comments to me. I had finally asked for help but I found out that the doors were already barred against me. Over the years, I had his friends ask me what I was doing with all of our money, question what pills I might be taking, and I even had a minister suggest I attend church to get a more spiritual outlook on the situation. What the minister didn't know was that Frank had been putting me down for years for my spiritual beliefs, mocking me for my attempts to live by Christian values of forgiveness and charity. By the time these accusations came my way, I realized it was too late to tell the doctor that Frank was the one abusing his prescription drugs, to tell his friends that he was the one spending our money, or to tell the minister that I was the one who had been trying to find a spiritual solution to our problems for all these years.

Some of the things Frank accused me of were truly ridiculous. He accused me of abusing cocaine because he thought I did not have enough nose hair. I guess it never occurred to him that a woman might trim, just like a man does. The fact that I had never abused this drug seemed irrelevant. By this point in our relationship, I had over twenty years of continuous sobriety, but I wonder what his doctor, and minister, and friends had been told about me. Keeping me on the defensive helped to make sure our real issues were never addressed.

While not a member of any organized religious group, I had been trying for most of my life to live by basic Christian values, and this also contributed to building the walls of my cage. I believed that those who had much were expected to share with those who had less. I believed that the strong were supposed to help the weak. I believed that those who had been blessed with good health should always have compassion for those with physical, mental, or emotional challenges, because, at the end of the day, "There but for the grace of God go I." Unfortunately, my attempts to help Frank and my compassion for his issues kept me stuck. Eventually, I found enough compassion for myself that I was able to give myself some of the help

I gave to others, but it took me many years to get there. I had to acknowledge that our marriage was gradually destroying me. I had to admit that even though I was very strong, the problems in our relationship were stronger.

At that time, I was studying a spiritual path called "A Course in Miracles." This path teaches that everything which is not love is a call for love. It teaches that there is never any justification for anger, because when someone acts badly, he or she is just expressing a need for love. This means that the only appropriate spiritual response to bad behaviour is love and compassion. I tried to hold myself up to this standard of behaviour, because I knew I had received so many blessings in my life. Working with the disadvantaged, I knew I had been a very fortunate person compared to so many other people in the world. My education and work experience turned out to contribute to my problem. I knew how to work with people who suffered from mental illness. I knew how to support people who struggled with chemical dependency. I was strong, I was resilient, I was compassionate, and I was flexible. I thought if anyone could figure out the problems in our marriage, I could. I applied all of my knowledge, all of my compassion, all of my experience to our problems.

But somehow, the rules kept on changing. Somehow it seemed I was doomed to fail. Giving up was one of the hardest things I ever had to do. It was second only to how hard it was to stay. While I still hold the same beliefs, I have also come to accept my own limitations. I believe the spiritual path I was studying is a very high path, and perhaps I have misunderstood some aspect of it, or perhaps I am just not ready for it. I have also learned to include myself on the list of people for whom I have compassion. I believe I am not expected to destroy myself in the process of helping another. I realize now that out of all the bars in the cage which kept me firmly trapped, my spiritual expectations of myself were a significant part, and this was one of the hardest barriers to overcome. I actually had to stop studying this spiritual path and explore another.

This is not a condemnation of these teachings, but a demonstration of my limited understanding of them. This led me finally to a different point of view. I realized that allowing Frank to continue in his abusive behaviour towards me was abusive to him. By continuing to be Frank's victim, I kept him stuck as well. Getting a divorce would set Frank free, too. The great sages and spiritual thinkers of our time have found a way to truly love their tormentors, and to not suffer. My problem was that I was suffering, and this meant it was my responsibility to escape the abuse.

This spiritual realization formed slowly over the course of several years. While this process unfolded, I did what I could to make things work. When Frank wanted to go camping, we went. When Frank wanted to go and spend a few days at a resort I agreed, even though we could not afford it. This kept the pressure up on me to work as many shifts as I could. I had enough seniority with my employer that I could have worked my full-time job, plus an equal number of on-call hours as well if I wanted to. It was hard to know where to set the limit. On the one hand, work hours got me out of the house and were often easier than being at home. On the other hand, since I was working a combination of day, evening, and night shifts, my sleep patterns were very disturbed, and I suffered from chronic exhaustion and sleep deprivation.

Chapter Six

Living with Dr. Jekyll & Mr. Hyde

The kinds of things which were happening at home were truly bewildering. Frank frequently put all pictures of me face down wherever they were displayed. Towards the end of our marriage, I started putting these framed pictures away rather than having to deal with this behaviour. Frank made continual references to divorce throughout our marriage. He showed up at my place of employment once with forms he had found online for filing for divorce. Needless to say, this visit took me by surprise, and I was deeply embarrassed by it. Even though he spoke to me outside, my co-workers were aware of the unexplained visit, and I had a hard time hiding my emotional reaction when I came back inside. Frank had a need for continual drama. I am not sure what the purpose was for this visit. Frank knew I was not at the point of wanting to file for divorce at that time. Was he testing me, or threatening me? I never figured it out.

Another enduring pattern during our marriage was related to Frank's wedding ring. He had asked me to put an inscription on it when we picked it out, and so I had inscribed "friendship, trust, commitment" on the inside of his ring. Shortly after our wedding, he started throwing his ring at me, sometimes from across the room. He said I was not living up to the inscription. Frank expected that he should be able to act in any manner he chose and I was not supposed to be in the least affected. I was supposed to be 100% open, loving, devoted, and trusting, no matter what he did or how he behaved. This was an expectation to which I could not measure up.

His wedding ring became lost several times as a result of his throwing it at me. At first, I would pick it up and give it back to him. Later I wound up just picking it up off the floor, and putting it on the counter or dresser. Eventually I learned to just walk away and leave it wherever it had fallen. One time his ring was lost for several months. He made comments indicating he believed I had it, but I did not. Fortunately Frank was there when I discovered it inside a Kleenex box where it had fallen, and he could see by the look on my face that I was just as surprised as he was to finally find it. If he hadn't been there, I would have had to endure the extra torture of him accusing me of hiding his ring, or calling me a liar when I described how I found it.

These emotional outbursts came out of the blue. I couldn't predict them or avoid them. When he became angry at me, after he was done yelling at me, he would then usually refuse to talk. I found it very uncomfortable to have discord and silence between us, and I would try to talk and resolve things. His preference was to let things sit for several days and then discuss them briefly in a dismissive fashion. These frequent periods of silence and discord between us were excruciating for me. Any attempt to resolve things would just make them worse. I would cry myself to sleep and suffer in silent emotional turmoil for days. It seemed that he always waited until I had become completely numb to the hurt before he would talk to me again. No type of emotional torture could ever have been more devastating to me.

This intentional cruelty on his part was one of the ways he could get to me. It was very destructive to spend days walking on eggshells in silence, and these types of conflict happened every couple of weeks. They were never about big things; in fact, I would usually be hard pressed to tell someone what they were about. It just boiled down to Frank being displeased with me for some reason, and I was punished. No matter how hard I tried to get Frank to talk to me to resolve these conflicts sooner rather than later, my efforts were always rebuffed. He would say he didn't want to talk to me until I was calmer. I would write him notes and letters, trying to explain and resolve things, but he would refuse to read them. He would crumple them up and throw them back at me. Although I shouldn't be, I am ashamed to say that sometimes I even resorted to begging; crying outside of closed doors, trying to get him to talk to me, but nothing I said or did made any difference. He would then twist reality by complaining afterwards about how he always had to be the one to start the conversation to resolve things. He complained he always had to make the first move. This was only true in that he would rebuff my efforts until such time as he chose to talk to me.

I had realized by then that my marriage paralleled the story of Dr. Jekyll and Mr. Hyde, the scientist who, when he drank a potion, made him turn into a monster. It often seemed like I was dealing with two different people. One was a guy with whom I shared several interests, the other one was an unpredictable and scary monster. When he was in Mr. Hyde mode, he acted as if I was his enemy, as if he hated me. The constant switching back and forth gave me emotional whiplash.

Other people were mostly unaware of what life was really like for me. Some were concerned that I worked too much, but they thought we were otherwise happy. My pride contributed to me perpetuating this facade, and I also desperately wanted it to be true. I wanted the family, the home, the son, the package. I continued to try to find ways to keep the peace and make the bad times disappear. Frank seemed to have a different agenda, which I eventually came to believe consisted of him perceiving himself as the victim. He seemed determined to make our marriage end in divorce, and I have since wondered about his possible financial motivations for marrying me in the first place. Somewhere along the way, he had realized that my family had some assets. He would exaggerate to others stories of my mother's wealth. He talked about my mother's jewelry, describing opening drawers in her home to find many carats of diamonds sitting there. While my mother did like jewelry, this was a gross exaggeration.

He also seemed to have no shame about accepting the money she sent us to help us out.

Frank continued to look to doctors for a solution to his dissatisfaction with life. He seemed to believe the answer would come in the form of some pill, and in me becoming a more perfect partner. The doctors gave Frank various medications for chronic headaches, including opiate based drugs. These complicated our situation because now I was dealing with an angry man with unrealistic expectations who was under the influence of powerful medications. He also began to mix these with alcohol, which he tried to hide from me. This added another layer of confusion. Mixing medication with alcohol was strictly forbidden by the doctors, but of course he was not honest with them either. It would cause unpredictable reactions. Once I heard him up at 2:00am in the bathroom shaving. When I asked him what he was doing he said he had a doctor's appointment. He obviously thought it was 2:00 pm in the afternoon. Being a drug and alcohol counsellor, I was sympathetic and tried to help, but then I would bump up against his hostility towards me. Sometimes it seemed that he resented my sobriety and my ability to work. I believe he would have liked nothing better than to see me fall apart, and he was actively trying to push me there.

To do so, he continued to prey upon my weaknesses and entertained himself through act of casual cruelty. I have one true phobia. While I am not afraid of snakes or spiders or rats or even grizzly bears, I am afraid of moths. Knowing that moths cannot hurt me does not change my abhorrence of them. Frank was well aware of this phobia because if a moth got into our house, I would ask him to remove it for me. One day, he gave me a greeting card for Valentine's Day. When I opened the card some type of mechanical contraption shaped like a moth flew out of it, straight at my face. I screamed for a few moments, and then I burst into tears. It had completely triggered my phobia. When I finally calmed down, I asked him what he had been thinking, to give me such a card. I will never forget his answer. He said he knew it would scare me, and he thought I would get a little upset, although he didn't think I would get as upset as I had. What was remarkable about his response was that he actually admitted wanting to hurt me with a Valentine's Day card. I guess by then wanting to inflict pain on me seemed to be an acceptable pastime in his eyes.

Years after our divorce, I got to know Frank's ex-wife, Mary, who lived in my neighborhood. She told me of a similar experience with Frank, which seemed even more devious and cruel than what I experienced. Mary told me that she also has a phobia; she is deathly afraid of snakes. She told me that several years into their marriage, but long before Frank's car accident, he toyed with her phobia, just like he did with me. He caught a snake in their garden, put it in a jar, and put it back on the grass. He then told her what he had done, and he furthermore advised her that he had not put any holes in the lid. He told her that if she did not rescue the snake it was going to die a slow, horrible death in the sun, and it would be her fault. He told her he had done this so that she would have to confront her fear of snakes and overcome it. He said he was doing this to help her. Now Mary is a kind and gentle soul, who would never willingly inflict harm on any creature. But she could not approach the jar in order to let the snake free. She cried and she begged him, explaining that she just could not do it, but he told her that was too bad, the snake would suffer as a result. Mary was distraught, but she did not feel there was anything she could do. Days later, she found the empty jar in the garden, and she could only hope that Frank or their neighbor had let the poor creature free. In discussing our similar experiences, we both believed that Frank tried to always give himself a face saving reason for his cruel behaviour, in this case "helping" her confront her phobia. It would be hard to definitely prove his intentional cruelty. He had left himself a plausible excuse. Mary and I, however, were both convinced of his malevolent intent. He seemed to enjoy our pain.

Birthdays were another vulnerable time. I always wound up in tears on that day. He would find a way to hurt me, no matter how much I tried to prepare myself. One year, he gave me a wrapped can of stove fuel as my gift. While I love camping, this five-dollar item did not seem like an appropriate gift, but I said "Thank you" and tried to accept it with good grace. He waited about half an hour, and when he didn't get any further reaction from me, he instructed Tommy to bring me my other gift, which was a set of lights for the garden. He then chastised me, saying he couldn't believe I had thought that the can of fuel was my only gift. I don't know what type of reaction he was hoping for. I just know I couldn't get it right no matter how hard I tried.

A thinly veiled hostility pervaded our relationship, targeting my fears and weaknesses. I have suffered from respiratory illnesses off and on my entire life, and I have a type of viral or allergen induced asthma occasionally. For this reason, I don't like anything that restricts my breathing. Although Frank never hit me, he did on a couple of occasions put his hand on my throat and choke me. This was always done in a supposed playful manner, but it was very intimidating for me. Coincidentally, Frank's youngest son Tommy also suffered from asthma of a much more severe type, and he used this intimidation tactic with him too. Once, when we were on a family camping trip in the summer, Tommy became frightened while playing in a deep pool in a river. He started to panic when something touched his legs and began to flail in the current. Frank grabbed Tommy by the throat and held him there in the deep water, ordering him to calm down. He didn't let Tommy leave the deep water until he became limp and passive. Frank then walked back to the campground, leaving Tommy crying by the side of the river. I stayed with Tommy and waited for him to calm down enough to be able to walk back to camp. I didn't know what to say to him. How could I explain his father's rage and cruelty? Wanting to protect Tommy was another reason I stayed in my marriage for as long as I did. Tommy had a forced visitation schedule as a result of his parent's divorce, requiring him to spend time with his father. I didn't want to leave him at Frank's mercy.

When we were around other people, Frank was always on his best behaviour. Other people were impressed with him, and I remember one of my mother's friends telling me how lucky I was to be married to such a handsome, polite, and charming man. For the first several years of my marriage, I didn't tell my mother anything different. We would visit her twice a year and I found out much later that Frank had been telling my mother that I was on the edge of falling apart and having a nervous breakdown, and he was the only thing keeping me together. This is like someone pushing you off a cliff, and then crediting themselves with throwing you a rope to help you back up from the ledge upon which you landed.

When Tommy became an older teen he made the decision to move to our house full-time. Tommy had reasons of his own for doing this, and I guess things were good enough when he was around, since most of our troubles were still hidden. This decision led to the best period in my marriage with Frank, after we had been together about seven years. I believe he felt vindicated because his son had chosen him. Tommy and I had continued to grow closer, and I was delighted to have him living with us full-time. At first things were OK, and Frank was on his best behaviour. Tommy and I would have long conversations about all manner of things, and Frank was supportive of our friendship. I believe at this time he was getting his satisfaction from knowing he was hurting his ex-wife, so he had less of a need to hurt me.

Eventually the bloom wore off. Frank and Tommy started to have power struggles. Frank seemed to set up some of these situations intentionally. He once put a strong fertilizer on the lawn and then watered it like crazy. He commented to me that Tommy was going to hate him for doing this, since mowing the lawn was Tommy's responsibility. When Tommy mowed the lawn, Frank complained about the edging. Because of the fertilizer and watering, the lawn needed to be mowed frequently, almost twice per week, and Tommy could never keep up to Frank's satisfaction. Tommy was required to do several other chores as well, and no matter his efforts, Frank would criticize the outcome. If Tommy vacuumed the floor, Frank would point out spots he missed. The tension between the two of them grew to the point where I was afraid they would come to blows. I was constantly trying to play peacemaker.

Just before the end, Tommy told me that if his father's behaviour continued he was going to hit him. I did everything I could to defuse the situation. If this had happened, I know that Frank would not have backed down. It would have been a contest of strength between them, and since Frank was a good six inches taller and outweighed his son by over sixty pounds, it would have been an ugly battle. Tommy was a young man trying to stand up for himself, but his father needed to dominate him in his quest to be in complete control of those closest to him. I was terrified of what might happen.

When Frank wasn't criticizing Tommy and I, he often left us alone while he went off and did his own thing. Tommy and I still got along well. We seemed to have a good understanding of each other and a similar sense of humour. We enjoyed each other's company and had long talks. Frank was pretending to be abstaining from alcohol, but I knew he was secretly drinking. I would find beer cans stuffed under couch cushions and in the laundry room. Whenever I found these I would put them away, hiding the evidence from Tommy and never speaking to Frank about it. I had learned that direct confrontation was only going to put me in a war zone, and I was trying to keep the peace until Tommy graduated from high school. What I didn't find out until years later was that Tommy was doing the same thing, hiding evidence of his father's drinking. We were both trying to protect each other.

I know that Frank came to resent my friendship with Tommy. He would come into the room when we were talking, jump into the conversation, and begin to lecture us on some aspect of our topic. Our conversation would stop and we would listen to Frank. After a brief monologue Frank would get up and leave the room. Usually at that point Tommy and I would look at each other and then resume our conversation, never commenting on what Frank had said. Frank appeared to have no idea of how intrusive he was. He never joined in a conversation; he had to take it over.

In the same way that Frank told lies about me, he also told lies about Tommy. After our marriage fell apart and Tommy moved back into his mother's house, Frank told Tommy's mother that his son had a drinking problem. While it is true that Tommy had done some experimental teenage drinking, he by no means did this on a frequent basis. For Frank to tell this lie about his son was a betrayal that Tommy felt deeply, and it left a long-term scar on their relationship. Despite my attempts to shelter him, I know that Tommy is the only one who really understands what living with Frank was like, since he experienced firsthand many of the same betrayals that I did.

Chapter Seven

Building the life boat

During the early years of our marriage my mother would occasionally send me money, and I would put it towards our household bills. She knew that with Frank being off work and then, later, on permanent disability, I was under a lot of financial pressure, and she was trying to help. After several years, I told my mother about some of my troubles with Frank. I also told her that it seemed as if the more money we had, the more money Frank would spend, and I suggested she stop trying to help, because I felt guilty about it. She told me it was up to me what I chose to do with her gifts.

When I finally realized that I might not be able to make this relationship work, I decided I might need to build myself a lifeboat. This was about six years into our relationship, when I began to get smart. I thought of various ways I could hide some cash from Frank. Years before, I had started getting my mail at a Post Office box, due to my short-lived attempt at running my own private counseling practice on the side. After I gave up my private practice, I kept the mail box, and over time, I made sure that I was the only one who had a key. This took a while, but I was eventually successful. Since my mother sent her checks to this address on a completely random basis, I started putting only some of them into my checking account to spend on our bills. I held onto some of the money my mother sent me. I felt justified in doing this since every cent I earned went towards household expenses. My mother's money was a gift to me.

Now I needed to find a way to hide it. By then, I had made two girlfriends with whom I had started to discuss my situation. I asked one of them to open a safety deposit box in her name at a different bank than mine, but to make me a signer on her account and to give me both the keys. I kept these keys at work. I then converted the cash into gold coins. At first, I was still hoping I might make this marriage work. My lifeboat was for just in case. Converting the cash into gold was my way of protecting it from inflation. Slowly, over years, and thanks to my mother, my life boat started to take shape. It gave me courage.

One of these two friends also agreed to let me store a few items at her house. I began to remove some of my most precious possessions to keep them safe. These were things like photo albums, pottery my father had made, heirloom jewelry I never wore, and treasured mementoes. I also saved precious documents such as tax records. I had to do this slowly so that Frank would not notice, and I spent the last year of our marriage carefully doing this.

Christmas was a great cover for me. When I decorated for the season, I took some things to my friend's house. After the decorations came down, I "redecorated" with items I could stand to lose. I had to be very selective, and could only protect a few items that were most important to me. Fortunately, my sentimental nature was not something Frank completely understood, and most of these items had no monetary value whatsoever. I had in the past experienced Frank destroying something I cared about just to hurt me. It was a card I had taped to my bathroom mirror which read: "It is better to light one candle than to curse the darkness." I considered this a moto to live by, and I had had it on display for years. Frank tore it to shreds one night when he was mad at me. I therefore did what I could to protect myself and my heart.

I also started talking more openly about my problems to these two friends. I needed a reality check. I needed someone to tell me I was not crazy. I needed someone to encourage me when I got too scared to contemplate leaving. I needed someone to tell me that I could have a normal life again someday. I needed someone to tell me there was an alternative to self-destruction. Mostly I needed compassion and acceptance. I felt so much shame, so much anxiety, and so much self-doubt. I needed someone who could understand that I had to find the courage to walk out of my self-created prison at my own speed. My best friend told me that she would love me and support me no matter what I chose to do, whether I left or stayed, and no matter how long it took. My best friend helped save my life.

Chapter Eight

Giving up & getting out

I was concerned about how Tommy would be affected if Frank and I split up. Since he was still living with us, I wanted to figure out how to do this in a way that would have the least destructive impact on his life. He was a sensitive teen and had always struggled a little in school. I believed it was essential that he graduate from high school in a normal fashion. I was afraid if anything disrupted him he might not finish, and that would affect the rest of his life. He was in his junior year of high school when I knew for sure that there was no saving my marriage; I had to get out to save myself. So now I started to play a waiting game. I still had moments when I felt affection for Frank, when I really wished that I could stay with him, but by this time I had realized that all my efforts were futile. I did what I could to keep the peace, and to run interference between Frank and Tommy.

Fortunately, Tommy was a busy teenager, and he mostly used our home as a launching pad for his many activities. I had real concerns about Frank's mental state by that time and how he would take our separation. Although he had made references to divorce throughout our marriage, I was not sure how he would react to it. He had, through our years together, also made references to suicide, and I was really worried that he might make an attempt if I asked for divorce, if for no other reason than to punish me. Since Frank had a fondness for strangulation, I was afraid he would hang himself in our home. For this reason, I felt I had to wait. Finally, halfway through Tommy's final year of high school, he told me that he had enough credits to graduate. Even if he didn't attend any more school his diploma was assured. Now I just had to find the best time to leave. Tommy was taking a class which would involve a long school trip towards the end of the school year. I decided that while he was away would be the best time to end my marriage. This way, if Frank acted out in any way, Tommy would not be around to see it.

By then, my relationship with Frank had deteriorated to the point where he made frequent references to divorce. For some reason, however, he wanted me to be the one to pull the plug. I remember him saying on one occasion: "Just do it." It was strange because he refused to discuss our problems like adults, we could not come to some mutually agreed upon decision. He wanted me to be the one to divorce him. I think this played into his perception of himself as a victim. I believe he also wanted to make me the bad guy, and wanted to be able to say that I had abandoned him. After we had taken Tommy to the airport for his school trip, I sat down with Frank and told him I just could not go on. I apologized, and gave him a written letter stating some of my feelings and intentions, and then I left and went to a hotel. By this time, my older dog had passed away and so I just had the one dog to bring with me.

Frank took my decision quite calmly. He had not been at all surprised and he began to pack immediately. We talked on the phone a few times and since he did not want to deal with the house and I had been paying the mortgage by myself for many years, he agreed to leave. Next began one of the strangest periods in our relationship. For financial reasons, I had to leave the hotel after a few days and we lived together in the house for over a month before he finally left. I had a trip planned to visit my mother, who was very sick. This worked well for Frank. While I was gone he backed up two moving containers and emptied out the house. He did not tell me that he planned to do this, and we had not discussed who got what. I came back and I found the house almost completely devoid of furniture. He had even taken things from the garden: flower pots, edging, even removing the fencing from around our rose bed, so that the deer would come and eat my flowers. He took everything of value, and left only items which were broken or damaged in some way.

It took me a week after my return from Alaska to get back into the house. He had led me to believe that he would be gone when I returned from my trip, but when I got back after my week away, I came home in a cab to find the door nailed shut from the inside. I could not get in. I left and went to a hotel, and I received a message from him saying how surprised he was that I had come and tried the door. I realized the games had begun in earnest. I contacted a friend who agreed to let me sleep on the floor of his extra room. I had put my dog in a kennel to keep her safe before I left. I collected her and I wound up staying gratefully with my friend for almost a week; finally I received a call from Frank saying he would be gone the next day.

As soon as I got back into the house, I called a locksmith and had the locks changed. I had to call in sick to work in order to do this, but I didn't want to take any chances that Frank would change his mind. Once I got back into the house, I took stock of my situation. I finally had a safe, peaceful place to live. I had a bed and a small assortment of odd, broken furniture, but the closets were stuffed with a lot of junk he left behind. He left his children's old toys, old school projects, miscellaneous personal items of his own, and a large pile of items he had been collecting for years to have a big garage sale. I have always had a practical mind, and so I decided it was a good time to have the carpets cleaned. I took the lemons I had been given and made lemonade. Slowly I began to rebuild my home. It seemed that things I needed came to me easily. A friend gave me a dresser. I found a matching set of plates at the local thrift store. I found it didn't matter to me that he had taken so much. I had control of my environment again.

There were, however, scars left behind. I had extra locks put on the doors by the locksmith, and I was compulsive about locking them. Even so, I occasionally had nightmares about someone pounding on the front door. These nightmares were very realistic and woke me up. I would check the house fearfully, looking outside through the curtains. The first time it happened it took me several minutes to realize that this had been a dream; I figured it out because my dog, who slept in the bedroom with me, was not reacting. It had to have been a nightmare. She would have barked if someone pounded on the door. Even so, my dog had scars of her own. She started showing a noticeable fear of men, shying away from them on the street, and I realized she had become generally fearful. I wondered just what she had been through all those years when I had been at work. Nevertheless, we were a comfort to each other, and we began to heal together.

Tommy moved back in with his mother when he returned from his school trip, but he did not take everything from his room. I packed it up for him and had a friend help me deliver his things. I began to box up all the things that Frank had left behind, everything that was not mine. I did not want to be the one to determine which items he or his children might want to keep. Frank had even collected a large pile of brush and garden debris, which he had left beside our house. This was waste material from our yard and also from our two neighbors' yards, which for some reason he had hauled over to our place but never taken to the composting center. I only had a car and no way to transport this large pile, so I hired a dump truck to come and haul it away. Slowly but surely, I began to dig myself out from what seemed to be literally a pile of someone else's garbage. I cleaned the house one room at a time. I started with the rooms I used the most, and transported things down to the garage. It felt so good to be free that I didn't mind all the work, I had renewed energy.

Meanwhile Frank had started a campaign to destroy my reputation. He talked to all of our acquaintances, and sometimes these tales came back to me. I decided that there was nothing I could do about it and so I chose to ignore it. This was another smart move on my part. I knew I was no match for him in this area; these types of battles are usually won by the person willing to stoop the lowest. I focused on the two close friends I had and let everyone else believe what they chose. What was funny about this approach was that years later, I had several people come up to me and say basically the same thing. They told me that they had had to eventually break of communication with Frank because it just got too crazy. I never really did renew these acquaintances, but it was nice to know that, in time, I was vindicated, and at least some of the truth made itself evident.

One area where the slander did bother me was on Facebook. Frank posted a long rant on my wall which started with: "My wife is a bad person" and went on for a couple of pages. I was not tech savvy enough at the time to know how to get rid of this post. One of my two friends was out of town, the one who had encouraged me to join Facebook in the first place. So I posted my own disclaimer on my wall saying that I was being bullied and so I planned to unfriend everyone and shut my Facebook page down. I left my post up for a couple of days, and then I unfriended everyone and made it so only friends could see my page. That was the best solution

I could come up with on my own. Years later, another person showed me how to delete that account all together.

Meanwhile I continued digging my house out, boxing up what Frank had left behind. It was strange; he had taken almost all of the furniture but left many truck-loads of personal items behind. It seemed he had taken all of our communal possessions. Perhaps he knew me well enough to know that his things would be safe with me. Frank had not yet moved into any type of housing. It was summer time and he was camping in various campgrounds. This was not due to any financial necessity; he had a steady $2,000 per month coming in on his disability checks. I think he liked the drama of saying that he was homeless. He had made it so that I was the one who had ended it and asked for a divorce, even though he had been suggesting it for the duration of our seven-year marriage. In this way, he could look like the injured party and thus garner sympathy. I began to realize how important this was to him.

Frank really needed to believe he was a good guy. He could not envision a relationship ending with two adults respectfully deciding to go their own ways. He needed one person to be wrong and one person to be right. He began telling people that he had been injured on our most recent vacation and that this was the reason I was divorcing him. In this way, he could make me out to be the bad person abandoning the sick person.

After spending a couple of months pitching his tent in various campgrounds, and even staying at a local resort, Frank left town. I was asked by his best friend Bob to forward mail to his house. I told Bob I was looking for somewhere to take all of the boxes of Frank's stuff, and so Bob said I could bring them to his garage, where he was storing other items of Frank's. Meanwhile, the furniture he had taken was being held by a storage company. I had by that time met a friend named Joe who had a truck, and he helped me immensely. Together we took four truckloads of stuff to Bob's garage. By then, Frank and I had both contracted a lawyer, and I was attempting to start a mediation process during which our assets could be divided without going to court. I was paying all of the bills associated with the house and the animals, even though the mortgage was in both of our names. I wanted to buy Frank out and my mother had agreed to help me. My lawyer, however, kept running up against brick walls in his efforts to negotiate on my behalf. We were told that Frank was unavailable and would be for some time. No one would tell me where he was, but I eventually figured it out based on information Tommy gave me.

Frank had checked himself into a long-term treatment program where they treated chemical dependency as well as other mental illnesses. Frank stayed there for nine months, and during this time I had no choice but to keep paying our bills and wait. He had forbidden everyone from telling me his whereabouts, saying he was afraid of me. He was still playing games. When he came out the negotiations resumed but got nowhere. He kept asking for silly little items which he had already taken or which I had delivered to his friend's garage. I kept telling him to unpack and he would find whatever he was looking for. I was so glad I had boxed up everything. He asked for tiny spare parts for the camp stoves which he had already taken. He even asked for some of the garden debris which I had hauled away, but I explained that this item was gone. He wanted the part at the bottom of the pile, which he called compost. I could not believe we spent as much time as we did discussing dirt, but he maintained that it was valuable and he wanted it back. It took several emails to convince him this was all gone. I guess he thought I would just helplessly sit and wait for him to come out of wherever he was hiding. He had misjudged me.

Meanwhile, our mortgage was approaching its renewal date. I spoke to my bank, and despite having a large amount of money in my checking account which my mother had given me, the bank would not renew the mortgage without a signed separation agreement. I was stuck. I believe this was the leverage for which Frank had been waiting.

When Frank left the treatment program I had started receiving emails from him. These consisted of rants regarding how hard his life was, and how badly I had treated him. I kept trying to redirect him to the issues at hand which needed to be resolved, but I got nowhere. He asked me for money. I told him I had a large sum of money just waiting to be sent to him, but I would not give him anything until we had an agreement in writing. At one point, he actually responded to me by asking when I developed a backbone. I couldn't believe it. I started to understand that for all these years, he had mistaken kindness for weakness. I had put up with so much for so long because I cared for him, I loved his son, and I wanted a family. I had also forgiven a lot because I knew he was sick. But I would no longer allow him to beat me up emotionally just for sport or as a way to vent his frustrations. He didn't realize how much strength it had taken to turn the other cheek for all of these years. Yes, I had had moments of despair, and yes, I had begged when I could not find any other way to get through to him. The fact that none of this had any impact on him had taught me something. I had never been weak, I had been kind. He did not know the difference. I was no longer going to let him abuse me.

I went to my bank and had several meetings; however, they still refused to help me until I had a signed separation agreement. I asked them if they were going to kick me out of my house since my mortgage had expired. They said no, they would just raise my payments, which would put me in a real financial bind. Frank was knowingly using our expired mortgage to put pressure on me. It had by this time been almost a year and a half since our separation. I had been paying all the bills while Frank played games. My lawyer suggested that I go and get a different type of lawyer. He was a mediation lawyer, and he could not take me through the court process. He suggested I hire someone who could. He referred me to a local lawyer who had a reputation for being the meanest lawyer in town, and the most effective. He was also very expensive, but my lawyer had tried for over a year and a half to help me and had gotten nowhere. I debated this decision for a while, looking at the finances and the ethics of it. I didn't want to hurt Frank; I just wanted a mortgage and a chance to move on. Finally, a friend said to me: "I can't think of any reason to bring a knife to a gun fight." Out of all the advice I received, this seemed to sum up my situation. My pacifist nature was getting me hurt.

I hired the big, bad lawyer and gave him the $5,000 he needed just to speak to me. Then things started to change. Frank's lawyer said that she would no longer represent him if he did not settle. She did not want to go up against my lawyer in court, and we were making reasonable offers. Frank left me a message saying he was not afraid of my lawyer, but he started making counterproposals. Finally we had an offer on the table. My lawyer offered him a proposal where I would give him half of the equity of the house in cash, I would take over all of our mutual bills, and he could keep everything he had taken. I just wanted out.

Frank, however, decided to send me a private and threatening counterproposal. He listed a long list of things he would do to me if I did not give him what he wanted. This included reporting me to the local municipality for various perceived infractions, including work I had had done on the house. He also planned to report various things around the house which needed to be repaired, but I had not had a chance to fix. He said these areas would be condemned. He said they would require the back deck, which I loved, to be removed. Another threat regarded trees which he had planted in the green space across the street. Now he planned to report this to the municipality, saying that I had done it, and have them cut down. Additionally, he said he would report me to my employer for various fictional misdeeds, including his accusation that I was abusive to people with mental health problems (meaning him).

The one threat that really got to me was his threat to report me to the U.S. police for various fictional crimes. He planned to cause me enough difficulty that I would not be able to cross the border until these allegations were proved false. The problem for me was that my mother lived in Alaska, I lived in Canada, and she was too sick to travel. Her health had been steadily failing. She was nearing the end of her life, and I had been visiting her at least twice a year. If he did what he threatened to do, I might never see her again. After sending me this long list of threats, he said that all of this would go away if I just gave him another $10,000 on top of the current proposal. I told my lawyer about this and he said it was blatant extortion, and that I should go to the police. My lawyer was very expensive, though, and I just wanted to get on with my life. I decided it might be cheaper to pay the extra and save on legal fees. So I paid the extra $10,000 and bought my freedom. I gave him a total of $100,000 in cash, thanks to the generosity of my mother. I was free.

One thing I learned about hiring a top-notch lawyer is that in the end, it was worth every penny. He wrote up our documents in such a way that there was no going back on our agreement. There was no way that a couple of years down the road Frank could come back and ask for more money. I was very lucky, because exactly three weeks after our divorce was final, my mother passed away. I believe she delayed her departure from this world to protect me, so that I did not wind up in a lengthy legal battle over my inheritance. I think Frank might have had his eyes on my family's assets from the beginning.

As part of our agreement, I had told Frank I would give him one of our two cats. Since he did not have housing where he could keep a cat, I told him I would hold onto it and Frank could have him when he had a suitable living place. This cat was a mostly outdoor creature, and when Frank moved into an apartment he asked for him. I asked Frank to reconsider, because I believed the cat would be miserable being stuck indoors on the 5th floor. Frank agreed to let me keep the cat if I paid him an extra $2,000, which I gladly did. Four years later, when Frank moved to the country, he asked for this cat again, and I let him have it. He never offered to repay the $2,000 ransom I had paid, however.

Epilogue

Free at last

The years since my divorce have been both challenging and rewarding. It took time for the scars to heal and some of them will be with me forever. I don't think I will ever marry again. I don't think I would ever give any individual that much power over me. Marriage is in many ways a business contract, and if your partner does not play fair you can lose everything.

Nevertheless, I have found love, friendship, happiness, and peace. I no longer have nightmares, and I no longer compulsively lock doors. I am actually back on Facebook again, though I have pre-emptively blocked Frank from ever contacting me. I know now that I am strong enough to deal with any bullying which might come my way. I have had no contact with Frank since he picked up his cat, and I am OK with that. Although it is not in my nature for love to turn to hate, I realize that it is not safe for me to have anything to do with Frank again. I wish him well silently from a distance, and leave it at that. He is no longer my responsibility, and what he does is not my concern.

I have also learned that what people believe about me says more about them than it does about me. People's reaction to our divorce was sometimes surprising, and I have realized that people often pass judgement based on their own beliefs and experiences, even though this might have very little to do with the truth. For years, Frank conducted a smear campaign against me in our town. However, this eventually worked against him. I guess people got tired of the drama and did not want to hear it anymore. Eventually, my heartache became old news, and the gossipmongers moved on to fresh victims. Because I chose to not participate in this verbal war, I did lose some acquaintances, but I realized early on that I could never compete with Frank in that arena and I did not want to try. I chose to take the high road and not slander him publicly, and I have never regretted it. Years later, I had people at social gatherings get up and leave Frank's side, and come over to sit beside me, saying to me only: "He talks too much." In this way, they let me know that they were not interested in listening to him badmouthing me anymore, and I am grateful for that.

My sweet old dog also found peace in the end. I met a man who gave her cookies every time she saw him, and he gradually won her trust and her heart. Tommy was deeply wounded by his father, and he refused to have contact with him for years. I think the accusation regarding Tommy having a "drinking problem" was the last straw on that troubled relationship. He has told me that his biggest fear in life is that he might turn out like his father. I wish my reassurances could convince him that he is nothing like his father. Tommy has chosen to not have children because he does not want to pass on his genetic material. He wants his family line to die out. What a sad commentary on his childhood. But he does have a long-term girlfriend, and he is happy and otherwise well adjusted. I wish I could have done more to protect him.

As for me, I have learned that what does not kill you does make you stronger, but that is not a reason to stay in the game once you know the other person is not playing fair. There is no benefit, spiritual or otherwise, to being a martyr. Finally, I have also learned that it is OK to ask for help, I do not have to face everything alone.